TWAYNE'S WORLD AUTHORS SERIES

A Survey of the World's Literature

JEAN DE LA BRUYÈRE

by Edward C. Knox

Jean de La Bruyère (1645-1696) belongs to the particular tradition in French literature known as the *moralistes,* writers who sought to elaborate an image of mankind in general. Like Montaigne, Pascal, and La Rochefoucauld before him, he chose to express that vision in a genre other than poetry, drama or prose, and like other French Neo-Classical writers he sought out a writer from antiquity as model and alibi, in his case the Greek Theophrastus. La Bruyère did more, however, than simply enrich the canon of man's foibles and aspirations. At a critical juncture in the reign of Louis XIV, he proceeded to inject each successive revision of his *Characters* (nine editions between 1688 and 1696) with a welter of details and realistic observation which yield a very social definition of men and women desperately attached to appearances as a means toward a status and prestige which La Bruyère reveals as hollow and self-serving. His subjects are essentially types, composites of observation rather than individuals, but he did free the character-sketch from the solely deductive mode used by Theophrastus. On the other hand, while his criticisms and some of his techniques are a bridge between the seventeenth-century figures of a Molière and later social commentary like Montesquieu's *Persian Letters,* his criticisms of a variety of types and social groups are definitely reactionary rather than revolutionary, a bitter summing-up rather than an idealistic call to action.

TWAYNE'S WORLD AUTHORS SERIES (TWAS)

The purpose of TWAS is to survey the major writers —novelists, dramatists, historians, poets, philosophers, and critics—of the nations of the world. Among the national literatures covered are those of Australia, Canada, China, Eastern Europe, France, Germany, Greece, India, Italy, Japan, Latin America, the Netherlands, New Zealand, Poland, Russia, Scandinavia, Spain, and the African nations, as well as Hebrew, Yiddish, and Latin Classical literatures. This survey is complemented by Twayne's United States Authors Series and English Authors Series.

The intent of each volume in these series is to present a critical-analytical study of the works of the writer; to include biographical and historical material that may be necessary for understanding, appreciation, and critical appraisal of the writer; and to present all material in clear, concise English—but not to vitiate the scholarly content of the work by doing so.

Jean de la Bruyère

By Edward C. Knox
Middlebury College

ABOUT THE AUTHOR

Edward C. Knox is assistant professor of French,
chairman of the French department and dean of
the French Summer School at Middlebury College. He received his B.A. from Wesleyan University in 1961 and the Ph.D. in French from
Yale University in 1966. He is the editor of
Rencontres (Harcourt Brace Jovanovich, 1972),
an anthology for advanced conversation courses,
and is preparing a manual of French expression.
His teaching and research in French literature
have been devoted mainly to the seventeenth and
eighteenth centuries, and particularly to style
technique as mediations of personality and
identity.

Twayne Publishers :: New York

Library of Congress Cataloging in Publication Data

Knox, Edward C
  Jean de la Bruyère.

  (Twayne's world authors series, TWAS 298, France)
  Bibliography: p.
  1. La Bruyère, Jean de, 1645–1696.
PQ1803.K5   1974   848′.4′07   73–15836
ISBN 0–8057–2507–5

To my mother and father, for getting me there
To George R. Creeger, for being there

Preface

In the last four or five years, a number of excellent
studies on La Bruyère have appeared, filling what was
a rather curious gap in criticism, given La Bruyère's
importance as a writer. There is still very little in
English, however, and I am grateful to the Twayne
editors for the opportunity to set down what I hope
will prove a useful introduction. I trust as well that
readers already acquainted with La Bruyère will find
a few new insights, but whatever one's familiarity, my
prime objective has been to delineate the modes of
existence peculiar to *moraliste* literature and to demon-
strate the cohesion of the work, its unity, and its
variety. While the chapters devoted to the *Characters*
may seem to reproduce the artificial split between form
and content, this is more an aspect of exposition than
of criticism and those chapters are intended to be
cumulative, assimilating what precedes them at a higher
level of the text, and moving progressively toward what
is most original in La Bruyère.

Professor Brody (see Bibliography) is virtually alone
in addressing himself at equal length and simultaneously
to technique and meaning, the resultant—which I call
"vision"—of a certain subject matter perceived in and
through a certain presentation. This is not an indictment
of less comprehensive or more specialized treatments,
or discussions written for a different format, but his
study (with those by Barthes, Kirsch, Koppisch, and
Van Delft) strikes me as the "best" on La Bruyère. For

that reason, and because I was able to consult his article only after my manuscript was finished, his remarks (on the function of inversion, on metaphor, physical presence, open form, and the importance of conclusion) were a welcome confirmation of my own conclusions. On the other hand, he seems tempted at times to see form as directly imitative of, or equivalent to, a certain outside reality. Among other differences, I chose to put greater emphasis on the *caractère* as an autonomous context, and have therefore defined observation as a more active function and placed metaphor in a larger and more continuous esthetic.

References to the *Characters* are made in parenthesis, citing chapter and remarks, e.g. (I, 1). Chapter references are separated by semicolons, and counterexamples introduced by "cf." The names of critics refer to their works listed in the Bibliography unless followed by a footnote. I have recommended in the Bibliography what I consider the most useful and readable English translation, but for critical purposes all translations are my own. I have also indicated the original in brackets where it seemed important and relevant, and have kept *moraliste* and *caractère* throughout for reasons which should become clear in the discussion.

For advice which proved to be as sound as it was generous, I am indebted to Doris M. Kirsch, Michael S. Koppisch, Jeffry Larson, Raymond Picard, and Louis Van Delft. I am also grateful to Middlebury College and the Ford Foundation for the time and financial assistance without which this study could not have been completed.

EDWARD C. KNOX

Middlebury, Vt.

Contents

Chronology

1645   August 17: Born in Paris, into modest bourgeois family.

1665   Takes law degrees and is admitted to the bar in Paris.

1673   With an inheritance from an uncle, buys the position of Treasurer General of Finances for Caen. (Thus acquires, with no particular obligation on his part, a title and an annual income. The procedure was customary at the time.) Takes up residence in Paris.

1684   Recommended by Bishop Bossuet, is taken on as tutor to Louis, Duc de Bourbon, grandson of the Prince de Condé, with residence at Chantilly.

1686   Sells his position as treasurer. After the death of Condé stays on as the Duke's secretary and librarian, with pension.

1687   First mention of the *Characters*, in a letter from Boileau to Racine.

1688   Publication of *The Characters of Theophrastus from the Greek with the Characters or Manners of Present-day Society*. Four hundred and twenty "remarks" with no mention of author's name. Overnight success, two more editions in same year.

1689   Fourth edition, 764 remarks.

1690   Fifth edition, 923 remarks.

1691   Sixth edition, 997 remarks, first mention of author's name (XIV, 14). Unsuccessful candidate for the French Academy.

1692　Seventh edition, 1073 remarks.

1693　Election to the Academy. Article in the *Mercure Galant* denounces sensationalism and judges acceptance speech "worse than nothing" (cf. I, 46).

1694　Eighth edition, 1120 remarks plus acceptance speech with polemical preface.

1695　Begins *Dialogues on Quietism* (published posthumously in 1699).

1696　May 10: Dies of apoplexy in Versailles. Ninth edition published.

CHAPTER 1

Introduction

WHAT we know of La Bruyère hardly goes beyond a sketchy chronology. He seems by all accounts to have been appreciated by those who knew him, although usually with reservations. A good man, but at the same time extremely sensitive, stiff and even testy, in the way those who are shy often choose to defend against an outside world which puts them ill at ease. Self-consciousness and a certain reserve were hardly the best temperament for his position as tutor, however, since the whole Condé family was notoriously ill-tempered, arrogant, and even vicious. The Prince seems to have been halfway sympathetic toward La Bruyère's task, but his grandson's willfulness resulted in recalcitrance encouraged by the distractions of social life, rather than diligence in his studies.

One can only guess at La Bruyère's reasons for staying on after his pupil's marriage. He must have had the leisure and the means to pursue his bookish preferences, and surely the intellectual contacts at the Condé Court were extremely stimulating. Whether or not he conceived the idea of his *Les Caractères* (Characters) as early as 1666–69, as his friend Brillat alleged, his position unquestionably would have given him an excellent opportunity to observe various social types and the range of behavior which fascinated his contemporaries.

Social historians frequently use 1685—three years before the publication of the *Characters*—as a convenient date for "the beginning of the end" of the seventeenth century. The Revocation of the Edict of Nantes, which had granted Protestants limited freedom of worship, is symbolic of the second half of Louis XIV's reign, increasingly marked by costly and unsuccessful military campaigns abroad, financial crises and destitution at home, and an aura of religious severity at Court.

A major thrust of Louis' policies had been to deprive the nobles of the power which he felt they had abused during the civil uprisings of 1648–53. This was undoubtedly due in part to what tradition has seen as unpleasant memories from his early childhood, but it is no less true that Louis' desire to create a modern, centralized state could find little room for those whose chief claim to consideration was birth rather than demonstrated competence and loyalty. The nobles were thus reduced to the status of cogs in the monotonous routine of etiquette and appearance at the King's palace in Versailles. The chateau was not finished until late in the century, so that in a sense it was anachronistic, a monument to royal glory which was already tarnishing. It was also a huge expense, although it now appears that the more permanent damage of establishing the Court at Versailles lay in cutting off the King from Paris and the people at large. Clever as Louis was in obliging nobility to waste time and money on sterile ceremony, he was nevertheless, to some extent, a prisoner of his own game, and his reliance on his ministers could only be as successful as they were competent and honest.

To collect the taxes to support his wars, Louis established a system of tax farms whereby an individual bought the right to collect taxes in the provinces, much the same way La Bruyère had bought a different position. The idea was for the state to collect twice, once when the privilege was bought and again in part of the receipts. The result, however, was widespread and ruthless gouging, considerable fraud, and reinforcement of the rise of the upper middle class. The pretentions of would-be gentlemen were founded not only on developing trade, but also on tax collection and loans to a state more and more desperate for capital. On the other hand, Pontchartrain's famous remark that "every time the King creates a new position God creates a fool to buy it," tells only half the story: It was one thing to laugh at them, quite another to keep them out.

Parallel to the social hierarchy an administrative and financial one was thus emerging. Where the former had its roots in the past, the latter took advantage of the course of events, neither with any relationship to the lower classes and populace but the vestiges of feudalism or a newer mode of exploitation. Too embroiled at first in daily problems, the royal administration proved unable to elaborate any major reforms. By the time projects did emerge, they were either shelved, like Fénelon's moving *Letter to Louis XIV* (1694), or banned outright if they did reach the King (Vauban's *La Dîme royale* [On the Royal Tithe], 1707).

No major writer until well into the eighteenth century would choose to see the situation as it was rather than as a means to express truth of another order (e.g. Molière). La Fontaine perhaps came closest, but the tradition and trappings of the fable, and the writer's social reputation, softened the blow. We shall see later that La Bruyère's attitude is far less forward-looking than it might seem on a first reading.[1]

The literary public of the time was a small part of the population, well up on the social ladder. In the earlier part of the century, those interested in such matters gathered at the townhouses of certain highborn ladies, in what later came to be called *salons*. Begun by women as a reaction to the coarse, barracks manners which their husbands had inherited from the previous century, they soon became the chief meetingplace for literary and intellectual discussions. The social revolution was twofold: working toward refinement on the one hand, but also drawing writers and scholars away from excessive erudition toward an ideal of communication which marks virtually all of the literature of the second half of the century.

French neoclassical theory was an amalgam of precepts attributed to and adapted from translations of Aristotle, together with *ad hoc* observations on the various genres and the relationship of literature to its public. Certain threads nevertheless run through the pronouncements and can be considered basic principles of which the rules are the necessary conditions. Thus the unities of time, place, and action were the means by which a playwright was to express verisimilitude (*vraisemblance*). The proprieties (*bienséances*) were a further guarantee of verisimilitude, assuring receptivity on the audience's part by not offending taste and by not exceeding the bounds of a legitimate probability according to the social code of the time. The writer's task was to express that which is "natural," although for seventeenth-century theorists *la nature* is an accurate picture of human nature, not the external reality of the Romantics or the Realists.

Aesthetic pleasure was believed to result from the avoidance of excess of all sorts, but this was a question

Introduction

of balance and harmony rather than a mindless moderation. A work should be regular, uniform, "reasonable," but not at the expense of intensity or tension. On the other hand, the literature of the period deals with passion and irrationality, yet Racine's Phèdre, for all her morbidity, still speaks consistently in twelve-syllable couplets. Similarly, the fact that one wrote about mankind in general, or a mythical or historical figure, did not preclude an individualized treatment. Finally, critics have shown repeatedly that works of the period contained frequent allusions to the contemporaneous social and political situation.

Those whose taste was sufficiently refined to appreciate such literary expression, a mixture of certain elements of the aristocracy and a number of cultured members of bourgeoisie, were known as the *honnêtes gens* (the well-bred). Their model, the so-called *honnête homme* (well-bred man), was defined by his elegant discretion, his taste, and his refusal to become specialized at anything, including writing. The Chevalier de Méré was the major contemporary theorist of the notion in his *Conversations* and *Discours* (1669–77), but the tradition runs back through Montaigne to Castiglione's *Courtier* (1537), and with variations in emphasis to Aristotle's *Ethics*. Van Delft has studied at length La Bruyère's criticisms of the affectation and superficiality of the latter-day courtier, particularly in relation to Castiglione and Gracián. What concerns us here is that the primary definition of the *honnête homme* was quasi-aesthetic rather than social, much less economic or financial; and that the late seventeenth-century literary world, in its relatively small numbers and clearly defined limits—its "enclosure" to use Barthes' term—

resulted in a situation where subject and audience often overlapped almost completely.[2]

This put the writer in a somewhat contradictory position: He was tolerated and in many cases even appreciated by the society around him, but never on a completely equal footing. Boileau and Racine were quick to accept royal sinecures at the expense of their writing, while La Rochefoucauld and Madame de la Fayette, the author of *La Princesse de Clèves*, both published their works anonymously in order to avoid the label of writer. Gracious and elegant living were in a sense as much the rival of art as its subject matter. This surely explains part of La Bruyère's hesitation to publish, and frequent references to writers in his work. On the other hand, part of the pleasure which the writer supplied lay in reflecting or refracting a certain social reality—not only themes and situations, but in many cases individuals, more or less adequately disguised: "I am [only] giving back to the public what it lent me," La Bruyère's preface begins. The writer was admitted to the social world on aesthetic grounds, yet the specialized nature of his participation was precisely what kept him from being completely integrated. All of which only sharpened La Bruyère's vision at the same time that it set him squarely in a major French literary tradition.

I   *The* Moralistes

Despite an abundant production of allegorical writing in the Middle Ages, the formative influences on the writers who have come to be called *moralistes* were their idea of Antiquity (Aristotle's *Ethics*, Plutarch's *Lives*, Seneca's *Epistles*), often as transmitted by

Montaigne; a pessimistic view of human nature similar
to that expressed in more recent Jansenist writings;
and the demands of contemporary society for subtle and
refined psychological analysis.

The Ancients were considered proof that there existed
a number of permanent elements in human nature which
were available for study regardless of the era in which
one wrote. Many of these commonplaces (*lieux com-
muns*) took the form of a conflict: between reason and
passion, being and seeming, thought and action, private
and public self, the momentary and the permanent,
etc. Such tensions were of couse well suited to the
dramatic literature which flourished in the seventeenth
century, but *moraliste* literature functions at a higher
level of abstraction, taking as its explicit subject mankind in general. "It is easier to know man in general
than to know one man in particular" (La Rochefoucauld,
Maximes, No. 436). In that sense, the *moraliste* deals
primarily with the conflict as such and only secondarily
with its manifestation in an event.

Moraliste derives from *mores*, manners in the largest
sense, although the word did not appear in dictionaries
until late in the century. (At the time they would have
been called "naturalist writers" or "philosophers.") In
French it refers primarily to a specific group of writers—
Montaigne, Pascal, Le Rochefoucauld, La Bruyère—but
includes other less important ones of the eighteenth
century and is also used with respect to certain works
by moderns like Gide, Sartre, and Camus. It is important to note that a *moraliste* is defined not only by a
certain perspective, but by a way of writing as well.

Not all *moraliste* literature functions continually at the
ultimate level of abstraction. Montaigne takes himself
as typical of the human condition, which means that

an image of mankind will emerge from an accumulation of specific observations about himself. Some will prefer to study human nature as it appears in others, or, like Pascal, construct a rhetorical model or type to be examined. (La Bruyère uses both the general and the particular, and at his most original places his types in a relatively precise and historical social setting.) The common denominator is the choice of mankind as explicit subject, and the recourse to a genre other than poetry, drama, or fiction: The emphasis is on formulation and generalization rather than description or illustration. One can speak of a *moraliste* dimension in the work of Molière, and certainly Racine's characters analyze their problems at great length, but what makes one a *moraliste* is the elaboration or adaptation of a significant form in which and by which to effect the ethical analysis. Essay, treatise, "thought," maxim, and *caractère* all deal with a certain conflict, but at the same time with its expressive resolution. The primary aim of the *moraliste* outlook is to analyze and thereby to understand, an ethic of lucidity which masters the irrational and the illusory by an ordered, i.e., aesthetic statement of the problem. It is thus not so much a question of moralizing or moving "from bad to good," as from ignorance and illusion to truth. If the latter is unflattering or unpleasant, the *moraliste's* major premise is that nevertheless it is always better to know.

Montaigne and Pascal both set man in a world of flux and impermanence, although the author of the *Essays* arrives finally at a philosophy of life in this world far more poised than Pascal's "man without God," whose frenzied attachment to things and distractions is a search for some kind of solidity. The frontispiece of La Rochefoucauld's *Maximes* shows a stoic mask being torn away from a bust of Seneca to reveal the real, wrinkled face beneath: "Our virtues are most often nothing but vices which we hide" (epigraph). Montaigne arrives at truth via a series of personal readings, while at the other extreme La Rochefoucauld's maxims are convincing mainly because their form orients and even constrains the reader's attention toward a conclusion which the extremely lapidary style makes inevitable. Pascal sought to construct the *Apology* on a series of ups and downs which would reveal man's true conditions as neither beast nor angel but both, a cluster of contradictions. *Moraliste* technique discovers man, shows him as he is rather than as he would like to believe he is. The *moraliste* is thus always to some extent outside man's fate, if only because he is writing the situation rather than living it.[3]

II *Theophrastus and Tradition*

Jasinski has documented at length La Bruyère's "debt" to earlier writers, and shown convincingly that a great many of his remarks, including some of the most bitter and seemingly personal, probably have their source in other books rather than his own life. At the very least, he was confirmed in his outlook by a number of predecessors, the most obvious of whom is Theophrastus. It was common practice among neoclassical writers to present one's work under the patronage of an Ancient: Aesop and Phaedrus for La Fontaine, Terence for Molière, Euripides for Racine; the corollary being that originality is a question of presentation and technique rather than innovation in subject matter. (Curiously, those who voiced the greatest esteem for the Ancients—Boileau, Racine, La Fontaine—have proved to be the authors most prized by posterity. The works of the "Moderns," men like Perrault and La Motte-Houdart whose doctrine of progress in literature is part of a general shift of outlook toward the end of the century, have on the whole been forgotten.)

La Bruyère was a staunch defender of the Ancients and showed no hesitation to become embroiled in polemics with his Acceptance Speech and its preface. His own presentation of Theophrastus, however, was something less than forthright. The first edition of the *Characters* contained one hundred pages of translation from the Greek, followed by two hundred of his own work. Nor did the use of smaller print to compress the modern characters mislead his reader: From the very first, the volume was snatched up for its allusions to contemporaries, and La Bruyère's successive additions consistently included the kind of satirical and polemical remarks which were the basis of the book's popularity. Today we may consider this a shallow reading of the work and side with the author in his disclaimers regarding the particularity and specificity of his remarks, but it is also clear that he was "using" Theophrastus as a shield. While his translation avoids the extreme freedom in vogue at the time, it is nevertheless based on a Latin version (Casaubon, 1592) rather than the original, and is full of errors and inaccuracies. Furthermore, it would have been more appropriate to refer to the English representatives of the Theophrastan tradition, whose work was translated with great success in France.[4]

All in all, and despite my own conviction that La Bruyère's work resembles the Theophrastan mode more than some critics have granted, one is obliged to conclude that he had recourse to Theophrastus as an afterthought, a guarantee or "passport" into the world of letters which would divert attention from resemblances to more notable contemporaries like Pascal and La Rochefoucauld. Be that as it may, and even if it had "all been said," (I, 1), La Bruyère claims to have made it his own (I, 69). What interests us here is how he went

Painting by Largillière in the Chateau de Mouchy

JEAN DE LA BRUYÈRE

CHAPTER 2

The Circumstantial Writings: The Characters

LA BRUYÈRE'S various preambles and circumstantial writings are not included in translations: *Discours sur Théophraste* (*Essay on Theophrastus*), first edition, *Préface aux Caractères* (*Preface to the "Characters"*), first edition plus major additions, *Discours de réception à l'Académie Francaise* (*Acceptance Speech to the French Academy*), 1693, included in the eighth edition, *Préface au discours de réception* (*Preface to the Acceptance Speech*), eighth edition. For the most part, they discuss a writer's public, one's aim in writing, the importance of the Ancients, and the relationship between the "manners of our time" and man in general.

Only about one-third of the Essay on Theophrastus deals with the Greek writer and his "credentials" as predecessor and model. Far more interesting in fact are La Bruyère's opening remarks, which deal with the pitfalls of writing for a public which loves to criticize and which is subdivided into groups ignorant of one another like the court and the town. Nor do all of one's readers look for the same thing: Some like definitions and intellectual rigor, others prefer an explanation via a mechanistic and deterministic treatment of the passions. Still another group prefers to see *moraliste* literature as corrective and educative, an application to one's own time of what is known about man and his actions. This is what Theophrastus had to offer and by extension, what La Bruyère is attempting to do: "I seek only to work within that branch of knowledge which describes behavior, studies men and develops their character." His argument for reading the Ancients is that "in a few centuries we who are so modern will be Ancients ourselves," and in a long paragraph he leaves off the theoretical pros and cons to evoke what later generations will have to say about the disastrous effect of money and new-found wealth on the then modern-day France. We should read the Ancients because we hope that succeeding generations will read us with the same interest, remembering that manners vary and so their portrayal must be constantly updated, but that man does not change in his heart and his passions. He is "what he was then and as Theophrastus described him: vain, deceitful, a flatterer, selfish, shameless, impertinent, presumptuous, gossipy, quarrelsome, superstitious." For all that (and somewhat illogically), Athenians were free, simple, and direct in their manners, and if Theophrastus never quite attained their simplicity his criticisms nevertheless helped them to better themselves. Finally, La Bruyère has added his own work "with an eye to pleasing those who receive coldly the work of foreigners or Ancients and who are interested only in the manners of their own time." He concludes by distinguishing the *Characters* from Theophrastus and various other predecessors (see Chapter 1).

A Latin epigraph from Erasmus' correspondence precedes the *Preface* to the *Characters*: "We have sought to admonish, not to offend; to help rather than wound; to be of good counsel to men, not to do them harm." He then goes on to reiterate in the *Preface* (as did most of the great neoclassical writers) that his chief aim was the improvement of manners. He states furthermore and rather ambiguously that the reader should keep his title (probably title *and* subtitle) in mind; "for even though I derive my subject from the French court and my own nation, it cannot be restricted to the court or this country alone without my book's losing much of its breadth and usefulness and without straying from my plan to portray men in general. . . ." The second half of the *Preface* is devoted to further considerations of how his book should be read, dealing particularly with its layout and the successive additions, and the various types of remark (maxim, sententia, argument, metaphor, parallel, comparison, anecdote, one-line observation, analysis, portrait).

La Bruyère's first two candidacies for a seat in the French Academy were unsuccessful, and his election in 1693 was due in great part to the heavy pressure applied by his supporters. His acceptance speech did nothing to heal wounded prides, since he went contrary to protocol in not having it published by the Academy, and had the nerve to say he had been elected by "unanimous" consent and to claim it had come about without his soliciting any votes. In the context of the Quarrel of the Ancients and Moderns, it was even more insulting to praise his patrons, Bossuet, Boileau, La Fontaine, and Racine. The latter in particular was the occasion for a slight on Corneille and his admirers, made in the presence of the older playwright's brother and his nephew, Fontenelle (who was elected instead of La Bruyère in 1692).

There are those who cannot stand to see him preferred to Corneille, the great Corneille; others, to see them equated . . . a few old men who, moved by anything that reminds them of their early years, perhaps most cherished in *Oedipe* [Corneille's *Oedipus*] the memory of their youth.

The *Preface* to the speech, even longer than what it introduced, poured more oil on the fire. La Bruyère moved rather deftly from a defense of the speech, citing the fact the public liked it and that he avoided *ad hominem* argument, to a character sketch of Fontenelle as Théobalde and a comparison of his adversaries to old crows which bore the reading public by "cawing around those who, flying freely and with a light feather [quill pen], soar to fame through their writings." He then develops at some length his refutation of the "keys," one proof being that he must have been writing about man in general since there were so many diverse attributions for the same remarks. Finally, not the least interesting aspect of the *Preface* is his explanation of why he had tried to be eloquent in the acceptance speech (such eloquence is out of fashion at the bar and no longer tolerated in the pulpit), and one passage where La Bruyère waxes eloquent instead of talking about it.

They went even further; assuaging with their critical zeal the pain of not being praised as much or as long as each of the other academicians, they went so far as to make specious and dangerous use of the part of my speech where I call upon all of them without being allowed to address any one in particular and where I make myself vulnerable by taking up the cause of literature, alone against their most irreconcilable enemies, wealthy persons made coldly insolent by their excessive gains or a fortune acquired through certain channels, and the favor of the great which money necessarily attracts.

In the original, one could almost be reading Rousseau.

CHAPTER 3

Modes of Organization

IN the preface to his acceptance speech before the
French Academy, published in the eighth edition,
polemics apparently forced La Bruyère to attribute to
his work an apologetic intention, and assert that ". . . of
the sixteen chapters, fifteen . . . seek to tear down the
obstacles which weaken and destroy in men the knowledge of God." The last chapter, however, is decidedly
the most derivative, even in a tradition where *moralistes*
borrowed constantly from one another. (La Bruyère
does so to such a degree that the chapter becomes
virtually a kind of second-degree observation of other
observers.) For the time being, La Bruyère's title and
subtitle—"The Manners and Customs [*moeurs*] of our
Time"—are an adequate and relevant indication of the
two basic categories in the work: the personal and the
social.

I *Passions and Contradictions*

In seventeenth-century ethical analysis, the heart (IV)
is the seat of the passions. Love is therefore a kind of
first-among-equals context, particularly if we take into
account its variants and derivations. It is sudden, violent
and autonomous, as the dramatic and narrative literature
of the time attests, and summons up corollary themes

of weakness and the passage of time. La Bruyère also devotes several remarks to friendship, which apparently appeals to him as a rare example of an interpersonal relationship free of desire. His remarks on the difference between friendship and love are typical of the ethical topography developed by the preceding generation, plotting on the one hand various reference points like love, friendship, inclination, hate, etc., and on the other tracing the dynamics of interaction among those emotions.

"On Mankind" (XI) is the longest chapter in the book, both in pages and number of entries. From the very beginning La Bruyère postulates a human nature at the source of our behavior. He never quite defines the natural determinant as precisely or as singularly as La Rochefoucauld, but the tableau is perhaps the richer for it, and in any case no more encouraging:

Restlessness of mind, unevenness of temper, inconstancy of heart, uncertainty of behavior: all vices of man's soul, but all different from one another. . . . (4)

Subject to his humors and his passions, man is variously indolent, self-important, or completely absent-minded. The stress of old age and the threat of death also reveal his fundamental weakness, his fragility, and lack of foundation. Selfishness, domination by the Self, means that the logic of the human condition is one of pernicious inconsistency and change. Not only has man no firm position from which to make judgments, much less seek a happy mean: His dependent condition of surrender to passion is paradoxically one of his rare sources of strength and initiative.

The world outside——others, circumstances—may also have a bearing on the self: "There are some vices which

JEAN DE LA BRUYÈRE

we bring with us into the world at birth and which
become ingrained through habit; there are others which
we contract that are foreign to us . . ." (15). Moreover,
man the social animal hardly creates an edifying spectacle when dealing with others. He is uncivil and incon-
siderate, fractious and even brutal. His avarice is typical
of his all-consuming envy and desire. Man consequently
tries to hide his essential vanity behind affectation, a
mask of appearances, and various other forms of
duplicity.

II *Between Self and Society*

Women (III) were a frequent category in *moraliste*
literature. Several of La Bruyère's remarks decry the
artifice and affectation of women, in particular the
abuse of makeup, an overweening desire to please and
attract men, to play the coquette. But women are
only the apparent subject. Age is a constant preoccupation of the coquette, but the passing of time is also a
topic of great human interest and importance. If women
in general are fickle and weak, they are also the occasion
for a very specific and biting satire on spiritual directors
and false piety. Women are a kind of touchstone or
privileged vantage point for the writer's inquiry into
intra- and interpersonal relationships, human foibles,
passions and weaknesses, the lies we tell ourselves and
others. In the tradition of the *moralistes*, La Bruyère
delves into a specific domain to study the dialectics of a
subgroup whose members delude themselves as they
seek to mislead others, but at the same time he points
up the failings of the male sex. ". . . they follow their
hearts, and depend for their behavior on the men they
love" (54).

Chapter V pursues a slightly different topic on the same terrain. "Society" is less broad than its modern equivalent, while "conversation" is somewhat less specific. Taken together, they refer to the social contact of which the way one speaks is a major manifestation. Strictures abound concerning usage, relevance, propriety, etc., but just as women suggest the general problem of appearances, La Bruyère chooses to examine language more particularly in the light of social discourse.

The very first entry poses the general and dramatic question of how to exist in society to just the right degree: "To have no character at all is to be insipid." The opposite of insipid for La Bruyère's audience is not forceful character, which is equally off-center (ex-centric), but *honnête*: well-bred, moderate, and flexible. In the severely limited social world of the time, conversation was a major means of developing and sharpening one's taste and intelligence. It was also a convenient way of judging such efforts and the people who made them. Moreover, as a writer La Bruyère is far more interested in characters who have some relief to them, and the chapter is a veritable gallery of the misspoken, the presumptuous, and the egotistical; Molière is more the predecessor than Méré. The problem, which La Bruyère underlines because the individuals are unaware of it, is not only how to speak, but whether to speak at all. "A fool is always an intruder: An intelligent man knows whether he is welcome or unwelcome" (2).

When La Bruyère takes Acis to task for not speaking like everyone else (7), *everyone* in fact refers to the *honnête* set (69). When part of the Court takes its cue from the common herd, it has been contaminated (71), and the same kind of touchstone is used to assess Cydias:

"He is, in a word, a compound of pedantry and formality, to be admired by townspeople and rustics, but in whom there is nothing great save his opinion of himself" (75). La Bruyère depicts a drastically limited community searching constantly for a common denominator to provide some sort of homogeneity. Several remarks deal with the problem of adaptability and social harmony, in families and in the provinces, excessive criticism and insincerity, the difficulty of privacy. Significantly, the author takes his observations even further, inveighing against those who willfully or otherwise allow such a state of affairs to exist, and those who suffer from it. The *Characters* is a book about the problem of social presence, and if the most picturesque examples are the intruders, La Bruyère is also keenly and critically aware of the intruded-upon, the other element of the dialectic.

Whereas Chapters III and V are astride self on the one hand and society on the other, "Personal Merit" (II) is caught between the two. "How very painful it is for a man who has no boosters and clique . . . with nothing to recommend him but his own remarkable qualities" (4). La Bruyère deals here with reputation and (lack of) recognition, and some of his most bitter remarks apply to an unseemly reversal of values: virtue is so rare as to consecrate those who have it as an elite, yet "we are living in an age when [titles and possessions] will bring him more honor than virtue could" (18). The chapter is an indictment of the self-centered and self-important, those who would arrogate to themselves a quality or status which is simply not theirs. True, specific references to late seventeenth-century France are not numerous, and the contemporary reader could of course always attribute craving after titles to his neighbor rather than himself. Other chapters to come, however, will provide a closer and more specific examination of social classes and types.

III Social Practice and Social Definition

A familiar topic in *moraliste* writing, "judgment" (XII) or more aptly misjudging, is the result of the pressure of others and our own lack of stability and autonomy. The ways of society, foolish social types, and the vagaries of reputation all bear witness, whether as cause or effect, to the absence of accurate evaluations. What distinguishes La Bruyère's treatment is the effort to adduce examples of the problem from the interpersonal and even symbiotic relationships observable in society.

Certain people are overlooked in the distribution of favors and cause one to ask: Why were they forgotten?, whereas, if they had been remembered, one would have wondered Why remember them? What causes this contradiction? Is it the character of such people, or the uncertainty of our judgments, or both? (1)

The corollary notion of the public, those who are in a kind of secondary limelight, may serve to reinforce the evidence of our misjudgments, or as a corrective, or both.

Fashion (XIII) includes eccentric collectors, dueling, social popularity, clothes and hairstyles, and religious hypocrisy; all of which are seen as proof of man's frivolity and fickleness. Certain customs (XIV) show a lamentable tendency to create and/or perpetuate social abuses, and the notions of custom and abuse are virtually synonymous in the context of the chapter. Nobility is impoverished and titles can be bought; much of the clergy is more sociable than it is religious; marriage is too often a financial transaction; money is a social disruption; justice and the magistracy are equally subject to the laws of self-interest; medicine and quackery seem to go hand in hand. (It is worth noting that these practices have a less explicit personal source than the fashions and are studied for themselves.)

The city (VII) is not so much Paris as the ethical space where one can see others and be seen. Particularly impressive is La Bruyère's renewed attack on the evils of imitation: ". . . affecting a character remote from the one they ought to maintain, [the young magistrates] become, as they wished to, faithful copies of very inferior originals" (7). Each group defines itself by imitating the one above it and mocking the one below. The futile and sterile social merry-go-round is motivated by the seasons or what one imagines will impress others, but always with a suggestion of a deeper, metaphysical abyss of bondage to others and flight from the self.

The courtiers (VIII) are equally other-directed, their preoccupation with appearances resulting in a falseness which debases moral values by placing fortune ahead of merit. They are less interested in the principles of virtue than in the rules of the game, and are obsessed with what it takes to get on in the world, usually defined at court as favor. Here too, the process is a rat-race of envy, self-promotion and denigration of others, and once again La Bruyère is severe with the gullible "public," those who have no critical perspective on the phenomenon. One is part of a hierarchical situation, reduced to flattery and to constant apprehension lest someone more important preempt one's place. Ethical slavery is the common social ill, and La Bruyère even takes the image of slavery a step further, assimilating the social conditions at the court to folly and madness (50, 61). The "social tyrant and martyr to ambition" is a remarkable portrayal of the creature caught between active disdain and servile imitation, who has given himself over to the court and no longer calls things by their right names (62).

Strictly speaking, the "Great" (IX) were the royal princes and highest rank of nobility, but La Bruyère is scrutinizing the so-called and would-be great rather than those who really are. A few remarks refer to noble birth, but this is often a reminder of an obligation unfulfilled. For La Bruyère actions are a more reliable criterion, especially since the problem of personal merit slighted and even unrecognized is uppermost in his mind. The arrogance and inaccessibility of the Great are part of a deeper complex of abdication of their responsibilities; moreover, their lack of involvement is an abstention from doing good, and all the more galling for their contemptuous attitude toward those they consider inferior. *Noblesse désoblige*, as it were. Here again, one of La Bruyère's greatest strengths is his ability to elucidate the sociopsychological mechanism, showing that the so-called Great cannot be studied apart from the interpersonal context. The first remark places the whole chapter under the negative sign of an overly favorable predisposition, not always disinterested, toward the Great. As strongly as he condemns the abdication of the latter, La Bruyère castigates those who relinquish the ability to recognize things and people as they are, themselves included. Ethical standards are forgotten when eagerness becomes gullibility, and there results a social symbiosis which feeds on mutual egotism and leaves little room for the inner-directed and meritorious.

This notion of public responsibility also figures prominently in the remarks on the Sovereign and the Republic (X). The successful monarch must be an inspiration to those who serve him, and know how to touch the hearts of his subjects. He must take careful stock of the various personal interests at stake, and the people in turn have their own duties and responsibilities. Significantly, the last word of the chapter is *great*, applied rather obviously to Louis XIV: La Bruyère is attacking social practices rather than political institutions.

Chapter VI is the severest of all such attacks. Elsewhere it is a question of the passions of mankind, or the problems within a more or less closeknit society: Here we discover a tremendous social upheaval. The financiers and tax-farmers are dealt with specifically, but the subject of the chapter is the *nouveaux riches* in general. Their humble origins matter less than their money, which is obvious from the number of nobles who marry for the dowry. The class is emergent, capable of "making its fortune" [*chemin*]. The repercussions of its social ascendancy are potentially or effectively harmful, as gambling substitutes chance for merit and religious life is contaminated. Symptomatically, *fortune* once meant one's social situation, a combination of what one is (or is credited with being) and a tinge of chance. Here La Bruyère not only uses it to mean a situation one has seized upon, but also takes advantage of its more recent sense of *wealth*. In other words, the subject is success and prestige through money, and we have come to the other end of the spectrum of personal analysis. Self is not inner-determined nor even socially defined by others: "Such people are neither parents, friends, citizens or Christians, nor, perhaps, even men: They merely have money" (58).

IV   *Structure*

A personal/social continuum is one way to analyze the contents of the *Characters*, but it obviously does not correspond to the sequence of chapters which La Bruyère established. In *moraliste* literature one almost always encounters a rich, complex, and more or less conscious interplay of levels and registers as well as traditional categories. Pascal's three orders of flesh/mind/heart are the most notable intrapersonal example (Br. 793; Laf. 585).[1] La Rochefoucauld saw "outside" activity and interpersonal relations as determined mainly by the passions, which are in turn a function of self-love. Whether or not La Bruyère's outlook is as stratified or as unitary remains to be seen. For the moment, it is quite clear, as he himself stated in the *Essay on Theophrastus*, that one can study mankind from any number of angles.

. . . [the book] seeks only to make man more sensible by examining mankind indifferently and with little method, according to whether the various chapters orient us by age, sex, and social status, and by the vices, the foibles and the ridiculous features which are part of them.

(See also Aristotle's categories, *Rhetoric*, II, 12.) This is particularly true, of course, if one's labels sit somewhat askew on the categories: is "Women" the same cross-section as "Mankind"?; do the Heart and the Court coincide, or intersect, or are they completely separate?; is "On Free-thinkers" about God or agnostics or both? Like all literature closely read, the *Characters* poses the problem of what the subject "really" is, what the book is "about."

Roland Barthes has suggested that in La Bruyère's

time one could still hope to write a *summum*, a book of knowledge in one volume (225). In that sense, it is not only useful but necessary that there be several angles of vision. Barthes discerns the following classes: sociological (the Great and the bourgeois), anthropological (women), political (the sovereign), psychological (heart, judgment, merit), ethnological (fashion, custom); and sees the individual in La Bruyère as the intersection of any two classes. La Bruyère does seem to be studying man in relation to two axes, the psychological and the social. What keeps the presentation from being a simple question of coordinates on a graph is that La Bruyère is also progressing higher and higher in society, at least according to the traditional vertical notion of social status. In the context of the work, Barthes' classes can draw one into comparing apples and pears, so to speak, since several different orders are functioning together, albeit not all to the same degree at the same time.

Van Delft discusses at some length the organization of the *Characters*, pointing out a first zone of inquiry, human nature, followed by the spheres of activity of the mind and the heart: art, love, society and religion, each one subdivided into classes, with society the largest such area (57). He recognizes that there is no particular hierarchy or precedence here, but compares the world La Bruyère is both reflecting and analyzing to a pyramid (64). His image of a cartographer is accurate and in sympathy with La Bruyère's time, although Mademoiselle de Scudéry's "Carte du Tendre" (*Clélie*, 1654) plotted emotional rather than social terrain. Similarly, his pyramid accounts more for Chapters VII-X than for the whole, which seems to describe a progression, at least in the chapter headings, from the personal (literary

efforts and personal merit) through the social to the King
(X) and then to God (XVI). Moreover, there seems
to be a radical shift between X and XI, and a shift back
to the social with chapter XIII. Typical of the dilemma
is the contradiction between Van Delft's vision of the
sovereign as representative of God and therefore both
source and culmination (64); and Goyet's (8), who
quotes La Bruyère ("There are generally in all men,
infinite combinations of power, favor, intelligence,
wealth," etc., XI, 131) as evidence that mankind is the
basic frame of reference.

This apparent contradiction is essentially a problem
of the critical reader's articulation of the patterns of
organization he perceives in the work. While acknowl-
edging the pitfalls of diagrams and geometrical figures,
I would suggest in preference to a pyramid the idea of
an ellipse. Rather than Van Delft's sixteen poles around
which the various remarks gravitate (63-64), self and
society are major epicenters and each remark is plotted
on the ellipse according to which of the two components
is more determinant. A pyramid would perhaps be even
more complete if its base were a graph representing the
two axes of self and society, with the height or level of
each remark being determined by the notion of "status."
In any case, it bears repeating that such representations
are somewhat arbitrary—if only because the time scheme
is absent—and should be considered suggestive rather
than definitive.[2]

V *Order and Sequence*

Time is crucial to the meaning of the *Characters*, not
only as theme, but as formative influence on organization
as well. A best seller in its day, the book underwent

nine editions in eight years.[3] Several of the revisions incorporated major additions, so that the number of entries nearly tripled—from 420 to 1120—while the length in lines more than quadrupled. Chapters I, II, XI, XV, and XVI increased by a factor of two, which is equivalent to losing ground as a percentage of the whole. (In the first edition, Women, Conversation, and Mankind were major topics.) On the other hand, Chapters VI to X and XII to XIV increased almost fourfold, representing a major expansion of La Bruyère's portrayal of social organization and function. As the work evolved, he showed a definite predilection for the concrete and the particular, but also for the current. The historical takes precedence over the general, the number of character sketches increases considerably, and the subtitle referring to the "Manners of Our Time" achieves, so to speak, equal status. (This is the primary reason why La Bruyère is considered a transitional figure as the *moraliste* tradition moves toward the eighteenth century.) Another obvious and significant example is the title of Chapter X, which changed from "On the Sovereign" in the first to third editions, to "On the Sovereign and the Republic" (fourth edition) and finally to "On the Sovereign or the Republic" from the fifth edition on. As Koppisch has demonstrated (12–47), later additions to the chapter (Nos. 23, 27–29, 31, 44) mark a definite humanization of the monarch as his constituency plays a progressively greater role in the definition of the social order.

Since the foremost influence on the book's evolution was public taste itself, the various adjustments and rearrangements were presumably not enough to bewilder the contemporary reader. Moreover, keeping the same chapter headings meant a loss of flexibility but maintained convenient reference points.[4] Within the chapters, there is an obvious attempt at organization: The first entries remained the same, and the first and last entries set themselves apart as more "important" or more polished. La Bruyère also very frequently groups in a cluster a number of remarks on the same topic, as "On Fashion" (XIII) demonstrates. One of the shortest chapters, it nevertheless tripled in size and there is a definite turn of the screw given to religious hypocrisy in the later editions. La Bruyère maintained the same balance between remarks devoted to fashion and those on religion-as-fashion, however, as well as their distribution within the chapter (1–15/16–31). Similar clusters can be found in all the chapters and even among chapters (I–II, III–IV, VII–X, XI–XII, XIII–XIV, XV–XVI), but in neither case is there any kind of outline form, with topics and subtopics, sufficient to organize the whole.

Even less sequentially, the remarks in most of the chapters are situated on various levels of generality, and there is definitely an interplay of general and particular truths. This is not, strictly speaking, a question of principle and illustration, but once again of levels and registers. Nor is the first remark necessarily the most general. (I am speaking now of the book in its final form.) The first four entries in "On the Gifts of Fortune" (VI), for example, underscore the notions of position via wealth and personal worth, but the fifth remark (which appeared in the first edition) adds a more generalized and analytical evaluation:

If one did not see it with one's own eyes, could one ever imagine the extraordinary disproportion which a few more or a few less pieces of money create among men?

This little more or little less determines one's entry into the Army, the Law or the Church. . . .

Structurally (social *disproportion*) and dynamically (*creates, determines*), the remark is at the heart of the chapter, and contains the tensions and upheavals of the time as La Bruyère saw them. The rest of the chapter will be devoted to the various modes of particularization in which he stigmatized money as a source of dislocation, culminating in the spectacular rich/poor parallel (83).[5]

Another principle of organization, governing both the general/particular relationship and associative clusters, I would call *modulation*. Laubriet compares "On Mankind" (XI) to a musical composition, with a main theme (human inconsistency) running through the chapter and a second theme of pity in counterpoint (511). Like diagrams, metaphors of musical composition, including my own, are frequent in literary criticism and not always convincingly necessary. Laubriet's is enlightening, although it is difficult to see what the 158 entries as a whole are comparable to musically. In other words, a chapter by La Bruyère is a series of remarks which are related but spatially separate, adjacent but less sequentially linked than two contiguous sentences or sometimes even paragraphs in a presentation in essay form. For that reason, *modulation* seems more appropriate to the movement—a kind of shift or skip within a continuous medium—from one thematic cluster to another, although the two metaphors are not mutually exclusive.

One can isolate a series of topics in "On Mankind": life and death (31–48), children (50–59), faults (60–62), vanity (64–72), others (77–85), qualities of mind (86–92), the passing of time (97–103), age (104–120),

viciousness and brutality (127–129), disparity and mis-
judgment (133–158). The "spaces" between the clusters,
however, usually contain a remark or two which belong
to both, thereby bridging the gap. Number 49 speaks
of the three ages of man; 59 deals with punishing children, 60 with learning from one's faults; 73–76 discuss
man's vanity in his relations with others; 85 moves from
judgment of others to the qualities of mind necessary
for such judgment; 93–97 shift from capability to performance, the last one over a period of time; man's
behavior in time (103) leads to the subject of aging;
absorption with self to the point of indifference toward
age and toward others (120–125) becomes more and
more pointed (126–129); two general remarks on why
man acts as he does (131) and the need for wisdom
(132) introduce the problem of evaluating others and
mankind in general. The last section can even be seen as
a preparation for the next chapter.[6]

This is not to say there are no gaps, although faults
and vanity (60–62) are closely related and the apparent
jump between 130 and 131 can be accurately described
as a shift to a more general level. It is obviously a question of how and on what level one defines theme.
Laubriet chooses the most basic and all-encompassing
in the chapter, and his presentation accounts very
economically for the reemergences which the successive
editions seem to have built into the text. *Modulation*
deals less with recurrence in the whole, e.g., old age (48,
49, 124, 132) or stoicism (3, 17, 23, 30, 42), than with
echoes and transformations over a shorter span, as in
the remarks on desire and happiness (19–24). In "On
Mankind," at least, it points up the ordering of what
might be called subthemes or motifs, although the two
muscial modes reinforce one another, particularly inso-

far as neither functions as a strictly logical sequence. *Modulation* nevertheless seems preferable to the idea of theme-and-variation because it explains how La Bruyère can group his remarks yet move from one to another, rather than simply positing a theme (as in a title or first remark) to be used and reused throughout a chapter.

VI *Intersection and Simultaneity*

Beyond individual chapters, the fact that the book was composed over a series of editions has left other traces. Topics cross over chapter lines and an index to cross-references is a much better guide to the substance of the work than is its table of contents. For every group which, like the partisans (VI, 13–35, 37, 55, 56), has a relatively hard outline and is easily circumscribed, there are others whose presence is more diffuse.[7] Money and riches, for example, are not limited to "Gifts of Fortune." Conversely, in many cases where money is at stake, there are observations on ambition, although ambition is not exclusively attached to the subject of money or even wealth. And so forth and so on.[8] We have already seen that La Bruyère is often talking about two things at once. Spiritual directors, for instance, appear in three different chapters (III, 36–42; XI, 61; XIV, 27, 28), and on at least one occasion La Bruyère refers to the same kind of thematic multivalence in a way that sheds light on the whole process: "It is also true that he wears breeches and a hat . . . which is why I have not put him in the chapter on women" (XIII, 14).

Far more important than the changes in the shape of the work over successive editions is the way in which this temporal dimension survived within the work and became part of its meaning. The *Characters* is neither a philosophical disquisition on ethics nor a scholastic treatise. It is a mass of remarks collected primarily on an additive principle somewhat reminiscent of a Montaigne essay, but without the overriding thematic presence of the self which unifies the later *Essays*. Faced with the proliferation of motifs, why not examine their intersections as a kind of motif or theme which is more than equal in importance to the sum of the various topics?

As Kuentz has pointed out in his edition, one moves closer to the core of the work via major themes than by relying on chapter headings which simply take over traditional *moraliste* categories (245–247). He notes six such themes: personal merit; (disdain of) wealth; virtue; nature (as opposed to artifice); a predilection for the archaic; and praise of the King. Every reader will probably have his own list of such themes, particularly since Kuentz seems disinclined to establish a hierarchy or even distinguish among key words, themes, and process vs. substance. Generally speaking, there are themes which are "historical," part of the *moraliste* tradition or the social commentary of the time: love and the heart, women, the powers of deception (*puissances trompeuses*), the court, religious hypocrisy, parvenus, social eccentricity. A second group is more specific to the book itself, adapted and emphasized in such a way as to be personal if not exclusive, e.g., merit, wealth, favor, infirmity and death. Finally, basic notions like *code* and *integrity* can be found not only in word-themes but implicitly in forms and relationships as well. They constitute the densest intersections mentioned above, and because they are major unifying elements in La Bruyère's vision, I discuss them in Chapter IV.[9]

In a work like the *Characters,* the subject or subjects—
not to mention structure—can only be defined by taking
into account the material-and-presentation as a functioning whole, a project which is complicated by the discontinuous presentation in separate remarks. For the
time being, the crucial organization principle seems to
be *simultaneity.* Whether or not La Bruyère sought such
a result, the book evolved so as to eliminate a logical or
sequential procedure, and consequently the possibility
of a meaning elaborated deductively. On the contrary,
given the work as it is, all of the remarks must willy-
nilly be considered true, and at the same time.[10] It is
probably more appropriate to speak of a certain logic in
the *Characters* than of its structure: Its organization is
simultaneous and diffuse, "suspensive" rather than linear,
progressive, or symmetrical. In that respect, the *Characters* resembles La Rochefoucauld's *Maximes,* which
give the impression that the contradictions and inconsistencies among the myriad discrete observations are
part of the subject rather than inherent in the genre.
In *moraliste* writing, the impulse to generalize falls
short of the statistical quantifications which are a more
familiar mode for the twentieth-century reader. The
accumulation of semi-isolated remarks leads to a kind
of tunnel vision, a selective verification of truth which
is more concerned with the validity of a given remark,
however particular or general, than with the possible
exceptions. (With the proviso, of course, that other
remarks may reverse the proportions.) This attention
to the point at hand at the possible expense of consistency and applicability to the general field of inquiry
is what makes it difficult to account for organization as
a whole and what necessitates a closer look at the modes
of presentation in the individual remarks.

CHAPTER 4

Modes of Presentation

L A BRUYÈRE distinguishes his own technique from Theophrastus', whose "myriad external details oblige the reader to go back to the source of a character's disorder," whereas his own, "displaying people's thoughts, feelings and movements, uncover the principle of their misdeeds and weaknesses, easily lead one to foresee all that mankind is capable of saying or doing . . ." (*Essay on Theophrastus*). It is not only unusual that he should discuss technique, but unfortunate that he should not make the distinction more clearly. All of Theophrastus' characters follow the same pattern: the name of the vice or representative type, then a definition in the first sentence, followed by a series of typical activities. Rather than going back to the source, it is the given from which the various practices flow. Be that as it may, La Bruyère is right when he states at the end of his Preface that his own material is presented in a variety of forms and figures of speech, and his reference to his own work probably concerned the character sketches rather than the more abstract generic models such as the definition or the maxim.

He is also properly aware of his debt to more contemporary writers. In the same passage he refers rather self-consciously to the practitioners of the maxim, i.e., La Rochefoucauld, and in the *Essay* he mentions Pascal ("the involvement of the author . . . reveals the soul . . . and seeks to make men more Christian") and La Rochefoucauld ("noting that self-love is the cause of all men's faults, he attacks it relentlessly"). Neither writer appears in name, but readers undoubtedly recognized them immediately. One should also remember that his contemporaries were far better acquainted than we are today with the voluminous *moraliste* tradition, which inevitably furnished La Bruyère with a certain number of models and devices.

I *Tradition*

The *definition* is reminiscent of Theophrastus, but was also a mainstay of seventeenth-century ethical analysis. In its most typical form, one noun is stated to be the equivalent of another or of a particular activity; the verb *to be* usually serves as the pivot of the equation: "A weak woman is one who is blamed for a mistake in conduct, and who blames herself for it" (III, 23). The typical form, however, is essentially a hypothetical model and admits of a large number of variants in the text, e.g., the negative (XIII, 2), inversion (XIII, 1), the equating of two infinitives (IV, 40), etc. All are examples of the inflection or expansion of basic formulas and patterns which characterizes the variety of La Bruyère's presentation. He also shares the predilection of the social circles of his time for definition by contrast. The parallel between Corneille and Racine (I, 54) is the best-known example as applied to individuals, but the *Characters* is full of analogies and parallels, whether the terms of the comparison be emotions, qualities, types, or individuals.[1]

The maxim reduces a truth to its densest and most

general expression (*veritas maxima*). Here, one wrote inevitably in the shadow of La Rochefoucauld, but the urge to try one's hand must have been irresistible. Many of La Bruyère's are not unworthy of the master:

If we are ordinarily quite moved by rare things, why does virtue affect us so little? (II, 20); Few women are so perfect as to keep a man from regretting at least once a day that he is married, or from envying the man who is not (III, 78); Our love affairs die from boredom and disdain, and forgetfulness lays them to rest (IV, 32).

It is perhaps even more interesting that, of the fifty-odd maxims, the great majority appear in the chapters on women, the emotions, and mankind.[2] This conjunction of commonplace and presentation is what places Chapters III, IV, and XI in the *moraliste* tradition.

The same is true of the Pascalian echoes. Like the *Pensées* (*Thoughts*), they run from the terse and elliptical, an example of which is quoted by La Bruyère (VIII, 80), to a middling length which might be called observations or reflections, reminiscent of but not equal to the best and most typical in Pascal.

A heap of epithets, inferior praise (1, 13); With many men, only their name accounts for something. When you see them up close, they are less than nothing; from afar, they are deceptive (II, 2); We seek our happiness outside ourselves, and in the opinion of other men, whom we know to be flatterers, insincere, unjust, full of envy, whim and prejudice. What folly! (XI, 76); Religious belief is true or it is false: if it is but a vain fiction, sixty years of living have been wasted by the good man, the Carthusian, and the hermit: that is all they risk losing. But if it is founded on truth itself, what a horrible misfortune for the wicked man . . . (XVI, 35).

[49]

For the most part they occur in Chapters XI, XII, and XVI. Partly for that reason the latter, as already mentioned, is the most tradition-bound and derivative in the work, although it is only fair to note that in many cases Pascal himself was relying heavily on Montaigne.[3]

Concerning the various other generic types, the author himself speaks of a fragment (XII, 28), uses capital letters (XII, 106) to convey the impression of an inscription, and does a pastiche of Montaigne (V, 30). Several other forms are less explicit but no less obvious: epigram (I, 46; XIII, 21; XIV, 23), parable (X, 29), fable (XI, 119, 135), vignette or news item (V, 9, 39, 47), even a narration (III, 81). A certain number of remarks could be called essays, albeit diminutive, in the sense of expositions of a subject.[4] Finally, La Bruyère shows a definite oratorical penchant: Two of his remarks are veritable funeral orations (II, 32; X, 9), and several so resemble sermons as to make him seem a moralizer rather than a *moraliste*.[5] The variety which impressed his first readers is virtually a mode of presentation in itself, and La Bruyère's gift and predilection for imitation indicate a personal trait which goes beyond a question of literary history or influence.

II *Portrait, Character and* Caractère

The portrait, one of the great literary fads of the previous generation, was usually based on an individual and presented a series of traits or qualities in parallel fashion, proceeding from the physical to the psychological. Depending on the genre in which it appeared (novel, memoirs, sermon, satire, or in isolation), it ran the gamut from description to moral exemplum, and from idealization to caricature. Latin rhetoric distinguished as follows between *portrait* and *character*:

Portrayal consists in representing and depicting in words clearly enough for recognition the bodily form of some person.
Character delineation consists in describing a person's character by the definite signs which, like distinctive marks, are attributes of that character. . . . [6]

On one hand, an individual in his physical appearance, to which seventeenth-century French writers will add ethical analysis; on the other, emphasis on the distinctive and typical.

Formally and generically, La Bruyère's remarks belong to the Theophrastan mode, bolstered by translations from the English tradition and adapted to the literary climate of his time. Until now I have tried to avoid giving a name to the genre for which he is best remembered, preferring to call it simply a remark or entry, precisely because so many lines of force run through the work. He himself refers to *remarques* in the first three editions; *caractère* appears only with the fourth. I shall use the latter to designate La Bruyère's contribution to the evolution of literary forms.

From what we have already seen of the tension between self and society, and the related continuum between being and doing or the virtual and the actualized, it should be clear that the word *caractère* in La Bruyère's title is far more ambiguous than its twentieth-century equivalent and even its English cognate. In its various contexts, the word may refer to personal psychology, force of character, moral fiber, characteristics, character-types or social role.[7] Moreover, La Bruyère often uses it to designate two meanings at once or the distance between two of the usages. Dealing with different but related notions and on different levels, it becomes a crucial concept, the intersection of the psychological, social, aesthetic and moral dimensions of the work. To go beyond the word and define the practice is to begin to understand not only the variety, but the richness and coherence of the *Characters*.

III *Observation*

Even a reader familiar with the literature of La Bruyère's time is impressed by the numerous specific references to clothing (II, 28; III, 29; VIII, 48). There are those who make a point of their finery and choice of elegant material (VII, 3; XI, 71; XIV, 16, 24); others seem more interested in jewelry (VI, 21), to the point of envying the trappings of a prince of the Church (II, 26). The wise man eschews ridiculous affectation (XIII, 11) whereas Philémon cuts a magnificent but hollow figure (II, 27).

A man at court and often a man about town, who wears a long coat of silk or Holland cloth, a broad sash worn high on his chest, shoes and cap of fine moroccan leather, a well-made and well-starched collar, who has neatly arranged hair and a robust complexion, who with all of that can recall a few metaphysical distinctions, can explain what the light of glory is and knows exactly how one comes to see God, that man is known as a doctor of theology. (II, 28)

Clothes do not make the man, but they are a convenient means for identifying him and especially for discovering what he is not. La Bruyère effects a reversal of values whereby every manifestation of a desire to impress and deceive becomes part of an indictment against those who parade about like peacocks. Furthermore, the organization of the work (*simultaneity,* p. 46) creates a kind of interference of one remark with another so that after one or two examples one can extend the interpretation to others and begin to look for trends. Thus, clothes can be classed with other elements of what we now call conspicuous consumption: one's retinue (VI, 1), a fine carriage (VI, 16; VII, 15), palatial surroundings (VI, 23, 78, 79; IX, 19). La Bruyère's references to food (VI, 1, 47, 63; VII, 4; IX, 28) and particularly to digestion as evidence of self-satisfaction (VI, 28; XI, 122; XII, 82; XIV, 24) are all the more striking for their rarity outside the novels and satirical poetry considered vulgar by his contemporaries.

Even more than clothes, cosmetics and makeup are the locus where the personal and the material, the dissimulator and the means of dissimulation come together (III, 5; XIII, 12). But perhaps the most treacherous and depersonalized of all is the way in which one's physique—eyes, walk, gestures—is debased into an expression of what one would like to appear (III, 2). Natural simplicity is lost as men and women seek out socially determined ways of being or seeming to be.

N** with his uncouth and imposing doorman who somewhat resembles a Swiss guard, and with a vestibule and an antechamber, needs only to make someone cool his heels there a bit and then appear with a solemn countenance and stately walk, listen a short while and then not even show him to the door: however inferior he may be, he will make others feel something approaching respect for him (VI, 11); Why does Alcippe greet me respectfully today, smile at me, leap out of his carriage lest he miss me? I am not rich, and I am on foot: according to protocol he should not even notice me. Is it not so as to be seen [by me] in the same carriage with a great nobleman? (XI, 74).

La Bruyère devotes two chapters to the art and importance of speaking (V, XV), and abundant other references confirm its position in social activity. Speaking is action, and just as it is worthwhile cultivating one's voice (XIII, 14) one can reap prestige by having the ear of a great noble (IV, 71; VIII, 16). Name-dropping is a prominent activity, and, failing the inspiration of illustrious names, one can always try to bluff via self-inflation ("a man of my station," VI, 21), extravagant use of the language, or even, like Théodecte, sheer sound production (V, 12). The only problem, of course, is that one may be found out. Some condemn themselves through their own momentum (V, 14), others by their incompetence.[8]

La Bruyère's use of free indirect discourse (*style indirect libre*) provides much more subtle irony. This is the device which "frees" an indirect statement by removing both the reference to a speaker and the subordinate conjunction. ("He said that it would be nice" becomes "It would be nice" or even "How nice it would be!") Its usual function is to bring the reader suddenly closer to the point of view of a character while at the same time maintaining a detachment which reveals, often ironically, the point of view for what it is. La Bruyère sometimes chooses to italicize lest the point be missed (III, 29). Elsewhere italics, like quotation marks, are simply missing: expressions like "only the public interest" (II, 10) belong first to the character, verbally or mentally, but are half appropriated, "liberated," by the observer.[9] In certain cases, the author even expands the device from one detail among many to a major element in the development, as in the long passage imitating the charlatan's spiel (XIV, 68), or to the whole remark.

It is bad enough to have to share one's religion and one's God with the populace: how could one possibly be named Peter, John or James like a merchant or a laborer? Let us have nothing in common with the multitude; on the contrary, let us underscore all the distinctions which separate us from them. . . . (IX, 23)

The religious skeptic (XVI, 22) and the name-dropper (IX, 23) are at opposite poles of presentation from the "dialogue" with Acis (V, 7), whose speech, like the references to jargon, is in fact indicted by the author without actually being transcribed. The point to be made here is precisely that there is a continuum, however spotty, of speech and speakers. It is not a question of opposing direct and indirect discourse, but of noting the variety of ways in which speech appears. Secondly, there are many remarks which combine more than one such device, leading the reader to conclude that a detail of speech should be considered suggestive and associative rather than exclusive. Finally, if various details make up the category of speech, that category in turn is one of the details of *observation* and characterization. The question now becomes how a *caractère* is put together.

II   *Juxtaposition and Extension*

The various details which were the subject of observation are often accumulated in series, creating choppy but regular sentences quite different from the ciceronian periodic form used and admired by other neoclassical writers, but reminiscent of similar enumerations in Montaigne. Juxtaposition, a mainstay of the Theophrastan tradition and a vestige of portraiture, presents a number of actions or ways of being (as opposed to accumulated detail). Generally speaking, commas and in some cases semicolons identify what I call accumulation, while semicolons and colons punctuate a series of verbal phrases, juxtaposed in the sense that it is less a question of rapid enumeration than of grouping together elements which are syntactically larger and which often partake of different categories or orders of observation.[10]

. . . one can hold out but a moment against a golden scarf and white feather, against a man who *speaks to the King and confers with his ministers*. (III, 29)

Like their Theophrastan predecessors, La Bruyère's *caractères* can be depended on: "A fool neither goes in nor out, sits nor stands, nor is quiet nor stands about, like a man of intelligence" (II, 37). It is significant, however, that the fool is illustrating the principle of those "inescapable mannerisms which give us away." The individual heaps up things, practicing extension from one detail to another in the hope of creating the impression of a character all of a piece: "He wears a wig, a tight-fitting outfit, solid-colored stockings and is devout" (XIII, 16). The *moraliste*, on the other hand, uses the *caractère* to show not only that type T will do 1, 2, 3, 4 . . . (n), but conversely that if someone does 1, 2, 3, 4 . . . we can begin to speculate on what type he represents. "Under an atheist king a professional devout would be an atheist" (XIII, 21). Combining the two procedures, one can say that as a significant arrangement of details the *caractère* is a question of "attitudes," in the sense of striking a pose but as outlook or "mental set" as well. The actor comfortably stretched out in his carriage and Corneille on foot both illustrate men's disposition toward literature (XII, 17).

Modes of Presentation

The very same fashions which men follow so willingly for their persons, they pretend to disdain when it comes to their portraits . . . they prefer arbitrary dress and meaningless drapery, whims of the painter which reflect neither one's bearing nor one's face, and recall neither one's behavior nor one's person. They love forced or immodest poses [*attitudes*], a manner that is harsh, brutal, foreign, one that makes a captain of a young *abbé* and a giantkiller of a magistrate; a Diana of a city woman and of a simple, shy woman an amazon or a Pallas Athena; a well-bred young man becomes a Lais and a good and generous prince a Scythian, an Attila.

One fashion has scarcely undone another, but what a newer one abolishes it and will yield in turn to the one that follows and even that one will not be the last; such is our vanity. (XIII, 15)

It is also a fact that the *Characters* contains very few "pure" anecdotes, events told from beginning to end without some kind of overt authorial intervention (e.g., XI, 35). In that sense, the *caractère* is faithful to the tradition of portraiture in which the present tense expresses a general truth, although the portrait was basically a series of static notations using *to be* or *to have*. Like Theophrastus, La Bruyère frequently places his characters in a kind of typical time, describing a number of activities in the present tense but in juxtaposition rather than sequence, thereby creating the effect of range and generality. The story of Arrias' discomfiture, for example, is apparently based on a real event. A closer look, however, shows that the anecdote is one manifestation among many.

Arrias has read everything and seen everything, or so he would have us believe; he is a universal man and bills himself as such; he would sooner lie than keep quiet or appear not to know something. [If] talk begins at a noble's table about a Court in the North: he takes the floor . . . gets

JEAN DE LA BRUYÈRE

around the geography . . . discourses on behavior . . . [When]
someone ventures to contradict him . . . (V, 9)

The talk at the noble's table is an example, a subcategory,
of his general character trait, and the contradiction in
turn a particular instance within that example. The fact
that the author saved the most dramatic and juiciest
morsel (Arrias' comeuppance) for last is only confirmation that sooner or later the character's negative potential
was "bound" to create a scene.[11]

In a number of *caractères*, the author extends the
character outside the realm of immediate observation, so
that the catalog of what he does in a series of presents
includes what he might do as well. There are at least
five constructions in the original which introduce or
express this kind of hypothetical activity: the *if*-clause,
inversion of subject and verb, "experimental" imperatives, the future, and the conditional. Curiously, the
parallel composition which seems to impel this extension
in time also reduces its conjectural relief, so that it seems
to flow naturally from the observed activities. As such
it underscores the consistency which is a major feature
of the type.

If one inquires of him what time it is, he pulls out a watch
which is a masterpiece; the handle of his sword is an onyx;
he has on his finger a great diamond . . . (II, 27, emphasis
added); *Let* Ergaste have his way and he will charge a toll
of everyone who drinks water from the stream or walks on
the ground . . . His is an *insatiable* hunger to have and to
possess . . . (VI, 28, emphasis added); Should a man be just
appointed [*Vient-on de placer*] to a new position, there is
a flood of praise in his favor, inundating the courtyards and
chapels, reaching the stairs, the parlors, the gallery, the
royal apartment . . . Let him begin [*Commence-t-il*] to

[58]

waver in his appointed post, and everyone very readily changes to another point of view ... (VIII, 32).

All are equivalent examples of characterial extension, and Ménalque is so colossal an accumulation that La Bruyère felt obliged to note: "This is less a particular character than a collection of examples" (XI, 7).[12] Theophrastus had used both typical time and hypothetical extension, but La Bruyère's variety of presentation makes for an intellectual operation which is considerably different. In addition to the deductive mode, there are many *caractères* whom we first discover in their behavior because the explanation of their conduct comes in the middle or at the end of the passage, if at all. Pamphile (IX, 50) combines all of the possibilities, but *caractères* like Hermagoras (V, 74) or Théognis (IX, 48) are simple descriptions. As with free indirect discourse, it is up to the reader to induce from the evidence what makes so-and-so "tick." "One should not judge men like a painting or statue, on a single first impression: there are an interior and a heart to be explored. The veil of modesty covers merit, and the mask of hypocrisy hides wickedness" (XII, 27).[13]

(The names of characters are sometimes didactically significant: derived from the Greek, Cydias (V, 75) refers to self-glorification, Périandre (VI, 21) is "above men," Tryphon, debauched (VI, 50), and Gnathon (XI, 121), a "jawbone" in action. Variants of Théo- are most often clerics, and Sosie (VI, 15), Crispin, and Sannion (VII, 9, 10) are names of valets in the comic tradition. On the other hand, while H.G. (I, 46) refers to a contemporary journal and P.T.S. to the partisans, N*** is used six times. The "keys" or allusions to contemporaries can be historically verified, but a glance at Pamphile

(IX, 50), which began with Dangeau, shows that the extension of the *caractère* and his hypothetical dimension are far more significant than a probable starting point or model.)

Generally, the *moraliste* leads the way, and if induction is one of La Bruyère's main innovations to the *caractère* tradition, he is also its major practitioner, rather than the reader.

> One has never seen them seated, never in one place or at rest. . . . They come from nowhere, they are going nowhere: they go by and come back again. Do not detain them in their frantic race lest you cause their machine to run down . . . (VIII, 19)

La Bruyère juxtaposes a series of present tenses to express frenetic social activity, and consequently his characters—despite their own attempts at extension or because of them—find themselves on a sterile, repetitive treadmill: "He will do tomorrow what he is doing today and what he did yesterday; and so he dies after living" (VII, 12). Although few of the *caractères* which do go somewhere are as explicitly enigmatic as (III, 36), as many as 125 remarks in all have a conclusion which is more than a natural outcome. The most striking example of juxtaposition followed by interpretive conclusion is of course (VI, 83): ". . . he is rich . . . he is poor." The *moraliste's* explanation casts a harsh spotlight, throwing everything into sharper focus. A large number, for example, refer to time running out or out of control, and even to death, as counterweights to the extension of which La Bruyère so disapproves.

Let us suppose that there were only two men left on earth, that they are its sole possessors and that they share it equally: I am convinced that there will soon be some subject of discord, if only over the boundaries (V, 47); At thirty, one dreams of wealth; at fifty it is not yet acquired; one builds in old age, and dies while the painters and glaziers are still at work (VI, 40); Titius listens to the reading of a will with red and watering eyes. ... There is a codicil to be read: it declares Maevius sole heir and sends Titius back where he came from, rentless, titleless and on foot. He dries his tears: it's Maevius' turn to do the mourning. (XIV, 59) [14]

(In other cases, the author adds not interpretation but a judgment, often criticizing those who do not choose to judge. See Chapter IV, n. 11.)

The rationale of his disapproval seems to be that extension inevitably becomes overextension. La Bruyère says as much when he refers to Cydias' overrefined thoughts and overwrought logic (V, 75) or social climbers in the clergy (II, 26), but he discerns it on a more fundamental level as well: "Folly . . . is subjection to fashion when we extend it to eating and living habits, health and conscience" (XIII, 1). Unlike Theophrastus, when La Bruyère speaks of eating and life-style he means not only as manifestations of the eternal foibles of mankind, but how and what they represent in a particular time and place as well. Specific vocabulary—financial, juridical, even medical—is not so much jargon ridiculous in itself as extension and inflation of a personality in a very precise setting. We are witnesses to the spectacle of traditional and social types in ferment, coalescence and deterioration. The more we observe and pursue our investigation, the more disastrous the results: Pamphile is not a Great but an imitation (IX, 50); the financiers are not men, they *have* money (VI, 58); Théodecte cannot be distinguished from his host (V,

JEAN DE LA BRUYÈRE

12). "Affecting a character far from the one which is theirs to maintain, they become in the end, as they wished to, faithful copies of very inferior originals" (VII, 7). La Bruyère's recourse to the forceful rhetoric of hyperbole and metaphor is expressive of the dimensions of the problem. Théognis, for example, so exacerbates his own proliferation that he imagines he is in two places at once. "When he walks through parlors, he turns to the right where there is a great crowd, and to the left where there is no one; he greets the people who are there and those who are not . . ." (IX, 48). Likewise, the bourgeois swallow food for a hundred families in one gulp (VI, 47), eating is Cliton's life and perhaps his resurrection (XI, 122); impertinent jokesters teem like insects (V, 3), and whole families are born in a single night (VIII, 57). One's presence and identity no longer have meaning, but yield for their definition to the means of extension: A musician gets back into the case with his lute (XII, 56), Antagoras is an old piece of furniture (XI, 125), Diphile a bird (XIII,1). As is the case with the interpretive conclusions which "block" the completion of seeming narrations, so at a critical point the metonymic principle of composition—identification and definition by contiguity, extension of detail—pulls up short, absorbed and appraised by metaphor.[15]

Judging from the mechanical metaphors in the *Characters*, to ask what makes a *caractère* tick is more than idle colloquialism, although it would be at least as accurate to say that ticking makes a *caractère*. Furthermore, the metaphorical function in general is remarkably consistent in the work. The main sources of metaphor (machinery, commerce, theater, animals, sickness, enslavement) all refer in context to the process or result

of depersonalization. Society is a world where behavior is regulated like a machine rather than spontaneous, and interpersonal contact is comparable to financial exchange. Willing slaves are stricken with a sickness, men so lose their human dignity that they are taken for monkeys, birds, insects, etc.

The fool is an automaton, a machine, a mainspring . . . whoever has seen him once has seen him in every moment and at every period of his life; at best he is [the equivalent of] the lowing ox or the warbling blackbird: set and determined by his nature and even by his species. (XI, 142).

One could hardly find a better example of stylistic convergence. The various devices—type, hyperbole, metaphor, juxtaposition, the generalizing present tense—come together to show how a new typology results necessarily from the loss of self and human dignity (XII, 103). Using the convergence of a number of stylistic features outlined here (observation, juxtaposition, extension, hyperbole, metaphor, and conclusion) as a necessary if not sufficient definition of *caractère*, the most successful and significant are: Arrias (V, 9), Théodecte (V, 12), Hermagoras (V, 74), Giton/Phédon (VI, 83), the man of the court (VIII, 20), Théodote (VIII, 61), Théognis (IX, 48), Pamphile (IX, 50), Ménalque (XI, 7), Gnathon (XI, 121), Télèphe (XI, 141, the collectors (XIII, 2), and Hermippe (XIV, 64).

CHAPTER 5

Vision

FRENCH literature of La Bruyère's time abounds in references to a visual perception of things, and Guggenheim has amply documented the extent to which people are constantly under the gaze of others in the *Characters,* because they seek to deceive and impress but also because others are forever on the lookout for proof of their own superiority. La Bruyère's visual and theatrical presentation of the town (VII) is typical of his particular and explicit attention to the systematic aspect of observed appearances, and that dimension of the work which can be called *code,* meaning both a system of signs and an ethos.[1]

I *Code*

On a first level, there are of course a number of details which need to be "decoded" by present-day editors because, like archaic expressions, they no longer mean anything to us or have undergone important changes in their social significance. These would include, for example, certain references to personalities, eating habits, styles of makeup and dress, games, transactions, etc. Because their "encoding" is essentially a function of the passage of time, they do not, strictly speaking, belong to La Bruyère's *code* in the newer sense, although

he himself devotes several footnotes to this kind of explanation. Moreover, it is worth repeating that the consistent observation of concrete and specific details is extremely important in the *Characters* and a major innovation in the *moraliste* tradition. La Bruyère not only observes, however, he also establishes a point of view outside or above fashion and convention so that detail is perceived as the locus of a personal code, i.e., a stylized presentation of self to society. In a few instances he acknowledges the importance of manners (V, 31, 32; XII, 85), but he spends most of his time castigating personal eccentricities and more generally a whole era which has gone awry.

The most literal examples of *code* are titles: "by dint of fine names, arguments about rank and precedence, a new coat of arms and a genealogy which d'Hozier did not draw up for him [a great lord] becomes a petty prince" (XIV, 7). Self-inflation runs not only into the past, but also into the higher reaches of society (VII, 20), and even extends abroad: "some stretch out their French names with a foreign ending and think that being of good parts means coming from far away" (XIV, 9). We are already familiar with this kind of extension on which La Bruyère casts so baleful a glance, and Kirsch (86) aptly points out the use of the same verb (*allonger*) applied to names and to a team of horses (VII, 9; XIV, 9).

Another obvious code in need of interpretation is the "newspeak" which many parvenus affect. La Bruyère is as attentive to the hypocrisy of jargon and neologisms as he is to name-droppers and usurped titles: "good at everything, which always means . . . good at nothing" (II, 10); "to marry a widow, in good French, means to make one's fortune" (VI, 61); "the tannery which he

calls a library" (XIII, 2). The verbs of definition (*signifier, appeler*) emphasize the fact that we are dealing with signs which must be given special scrutiny if we are to understand what is going on in a society where things are no longer called by their right names (VIII, 62; XIV, 6, 73). In one of the bleakest remarks in the book, albeit as exceptional as those on etiquette, La Bruyère accepts a certain number of stock phrases about friendship because they are the *image* of the best in mankind and because men "seem to have agreed among themselves to be content with appearances" (VIII, 81).[2]

There is no need to rehearse here all the details of *observation,* the role of accumulation and juxtaposition in expressing and defining a consistent and frequent phenomenon. What makes it a *vision* is the sense of an observer or at least an observation point which enables us to move from description to analysis and judgment. In a few instances La Bruyère points out explicitly what is transpiring: "with all of that [he] remembers [to add] a few metaphysical distinctions" (II, 28); ". . . they accompany such extravagant language with an affected gesture" (V, 6); "his voice, his walk, his gestures, his attitude, all go with his facial expression" (VIII, 61). In the last case, the author has already compared Théodote to an actor arriving on stage, and it becomes more and more apparent that a character's system of self-expression is in fact a series of clues on two levels. The desire to distinguish oneself may or may not lead to social prestige, but in the context of the *Characters,* it necessarily results in self-incrimination. The code exists solely to be broken, so to speak. "Drance wants to appear to govern his master, who believes no such a thing . . . [all Drance's efforts]

are more the mark of a pretentious fool than a favorite"
(IV, 71).

The point is that if one's code is to succeed it must
seem to be a continuation, a simple expression of one's
person rather than a borrowing. The first and most
direct step in breaking it is therefore to show it up as a
code, a representation rather than a reality, and this
is the function of references to mask and theater. Theater
was an extremely popular form of entertainment at the
time and was also a conventional expression for social
function and drama. In fact it had been long before
La Bruyère and the notion of role-playing is an important element of modern social-psychological analysis.
What distinguishes La Bruyère's use of the device is
the sense of a continuity, which he establishes at one
pole by references to makeup, but which runs through
all aspects of his "presentation." The people he observes
are perceived as actors who arrive on the social scene
with schemes resembling stage machinery or masks,
and who hope to play a more important role than the
one in which they were originally cast. The field of the
theatrical image thus includes literal, conventional and
figurative *observation*, all sustaining countless references to seeming and appearances, enriching and com-
plicating the notion of "character."[3]

In a few rare but extremely significant remarks, the
theatrical image is taken one step further, and we find
ourselves in a foreign land whose conventions we no
longer share and which consequently have become
opaque. Some references express an ironic ethnocentrism
whereby customs which seem perfectly natural appear
barbaric to other eyes: gambling (VI, 71, 72), abuse of
alcohol (XII, 24), apparent worship of the king at
Versailles (VII, 74), the obligation of a bride to enter-

tain on the day after her wedding night (VII, 19). All are negative proofs that reason can be found everywhere (XII, 22), ironic indictments of "our" elegance (XII, 23). Still more significant are the remarks which see "our" world as not only strange but systematically so, a country where joy is a mask and suffering hidden (VIII, 63). The court is a new world (VIII, 9) and the town is divided into so many little republics, each with "its own laws, customs, jargon and amusements" (VII, 4). Extension and self-inflation have culminated in the establishment of coteries preoccupied only with self and the exclusion of the unwelcome or uninitiated. "[Even] the most intelligent man of the world, whom chance has brought among them, is a stranger: as though in a distant land, he knows neither the roads nor the language nor the customs . . ." (*ibid.*).

This man of the world embodies the *moraliste* undertaking to get at the meaning of the signs, and his very failure is an indictment, the positive foil to social exaggeration and abuse. This "representative" does not always fail, however, and a large number of remarks deal explicitly and even theoretically with successful observation. (Synonyms in the text for this decoding operation are *discernment, penetration, reveal*, etc.)

He who has seen into the Court knows what virtue is and what religious hypocrisy is: he makes no mistake about one or the other (XIII, 20); An old man who has lived at court, who has good sense and a good memory, is an inestimable treasure . . . one can learn from him rules for manners and conduct which are dependable because they are founded on experience (XI, 118); A man of merit is, I believe, highly entertained when he sees the same seat in a gathering or at a show which has been refused him given to a man who has neither eyes to see, nor ears for hearing, nor the intelligence to know and to judge . . . (VIII, 60).

The lucidity of the successful observer is in direct opposition to the blindness, conceit and/or favorable predisposition which La Bruyère defines as the miserable state of *prévention* (XII, 41; IX, 1). "Man, who is mind and spirit, is [in fact] governed by his eyes and ears" (XI, 154); "I open my eyes wide and watch them carefully; when they speak I listen; I inquire, and collect the facts I am told . . ." (III, 42; IX, 20). Observation and discernment also function at a higher level of the text, a level which is rhetorical in the sense that it involves a writer-seer ("I") and a public ("you").[4]

II *The Rhetorical Situation*

It was a commonplace of earlier criticism on La Bruyère to see the writing of the *Characters* as compensation, a kind of semiofficial revenge wrought upon those who ignore personal merit in order to assuage the hurt feelings of the author himself and to avenge the back-row seat the society of his time seemed to have reserved for him. Armed with his biography, it is difficult not to find traces of the personal and individual La Bruyère in his work, even more so than in the *Maximes* of La Rochefoucauld, the other contemporary case of putative literary therapy outside the autobiographical form. But the theme of the constraints of marriage and the freedom of bachelorhood (II, 25; III, 78; IV, 16) was part of the *moraliste* tradition and not necessarily personal allusion; the same is true of the many remarks on personal merit. Moreover, the only remark in which La Bruyère is explicitly referring to "La Bruyère"—as opposed to an elusive "I"—is an ironic one (XIV, 14), and that fact alone should put the reader on his guard.

The problem is one that haunts literature in general

and *moraliste* writing in particular: To what extent does an author exist in his work, explicitly or implicitly, and how does one identify him? It has been shown, for instance, that Montaigne, who sees himself as an image of men in general, cannot make general judgments directly since seeing faults in others presupposes his having got rid of the faults in himself; he is therefore obliged to establish two levels of discourse, the first consisting of relative truths, and the second as criticism of the first. La Rochefoucauld writes from seeming omniscience, a position above and outside even the small elite for which he leaves room in his ethic, but a position untenable logically given the considerable indulgence of his self-portrait. Finally, the fragmentary and unfinished nature of Pascal's *Pensées* long made it extremely difficult to evaluate remarks in the first person: Were they to be confessional, or attributed to the agnostic? His "and I who write this have perhaps the same desire" (Br. 150; Laf. 627) seems to reintegrate the writer into the ethical order (as opposed to the aesthetics of lucidity), but it strikes a solitary note and there is no guarantee it would have appeared in the final Apology.[5]

Admittedly, in many cases one can interpret pronouns too strictly, and to recognize a certain degree of convention is to reduce somewhat one's perplexity. Furthermore, the discontinuous presentation of *moraliste* writing—"tunnel vision" in the *Characters*—creates a semiautonomous context for each remark, facing, so to speak, inward on its own truthfulness and only secondarily an element of a larger whole. Nevertheless, the variety and seeming inconsistencies in the use of pronouns in the *Characters* is somewhat disconcerting:

Vision

One comes too late . . . but I have made it mine (I, 1, 69);
once you have put on the final touches . . . one of the herds-
men . . . (VI, 78); He never enjoyed it so fully or peacefully
as you do . . . (VI, 79); Some men . . . All our misery . . .
(XI, 99).

There are, however, certain strains which run through
the work or through a large enough number of remarks
to constitute major modes of alignment. *Observation*
is one, and we have seem how it is absorbed into a
semiology, or study of signs. The semiological function
is in turn subsumed into a tone or vision which has
many avatars in the text but which is a function within
the text itself rather than a distillation of biography.
Because La Bruyère uses "I" so often, many earlier critics were content with the biographical dimension, but
an expression like "a man born a Christian and French"
(I, 60) or a model like Antisthène (XII, 21), indicates
that we would do well to seek out the textual components of the observational function before assuming
La Bruyère is speaking as "himself."

On one level, particularly well established in the first
chapter, the observer is a writer, the lucid *moraliste*
equivalent of the omniscient narrator in fiction. It is
true that the first chapter deals with the act of writing,
but it is precisely significant that the author should
provide a kind of buffer area at the entrance to his work,
a transition alerting us to the fact that his presence in
the work is a refraction rather than a reflection: "One
comes too late . . . (1); What else can an author do . . .
(27); The *moraliste* spends his life . . . (34); All
writers . . . (56); If criticism comes from a man who . . .
(63)." Just as he does with the objects of observation,
La Bruyère refers variously to the subject (observer)
as part of a class or in his function, rather than in his

personal and temporal existence. The "I" is only one of many types of observer, albeit by far the predominant one. Even if on a few occasions he speaks like a proud author, he never abandons his activity within the work (XII, 93; XIII, 14). The reference to "La Bruyère" is ironic, the final remark ironically coy ("I am equally astonished"), and the writers of Chapter XII (21, 67, 101) are avatars of personal merit and analogs to other models (29, 55, 73–75, 78) rather than simple biographical substitutes.

In other words, if we establish the paradigm of equivalent subjects, the various forms of observer in the text, "I" is the most prominent, but the first person is also generalized and reinforced by a variety of other types such as the man of merit (VIII, 60) or Socrates (XII, 66). On the other hand, examination of how the "I" supports itself other than by a kinship to illustrious predecessors and homologues reveals a number of devices which converge to create a strikingly coherent form of vision. "I" is not only semiologist and writer, but orator as well.

The observer's tone—indignant, bitter, even sarcastic— is of course why critics have seen La Bruyère behind the pronoun, but a whole arsenal of rhetorical devices so colors the work that it seems at points to be preachment. At the most basic level are the corrections, specifications, and liberties of expression which are underscored for the benefit of the reader/listener. Furthermore, the remarks are full of syntactical devices suited to the rhythm of oral presentation—accumulation, juxtaposition, apposition—which in the case of the first and the last are usually negative and judgmental. Exclamations, often in conjunction with appositives, express similar indignation. "Other times, other manners (III,

43); a disgrace to mankind (XI, 27). Finally, at the level of address, rhetorical questions and apostrophe establish a public in the *Characters*.[6] "What is a woman who is 'directed'? (III, 36); Who would have doubted? (XI, 104); Was he not afraid of dying? (XI, 120); Are you serious? (II, 18); cry out to those pious hypocrites (III, 40); Flee, withdraw: you are not far enough away" (VI, 35). In other words, if La Bruyère the man and the author wrote for his contemporaries, the "I" is speaking to implicit listeners, whether or not the readers identified themselves with that rhetorical audience. Furthermore, the orator is calling on those listeners to consider the basic topic of *moraliste* literature, the human condition. The rhetorical situation of the work can be represented thus:

La Bruyère ["I" > mankind < "you"] readers

We have already seen that tunnel vision works to maintain a certain elasticity in the real and theoretical boundaries of "mankind," but the importance of such variations to the vision and meaning of the work becomes clearer as we map out its rhetorical situation. Critical observation is the common denominator within that variety. It is essential to note that when the "I" participates in mankind, it is usually as exemplar rather than failure. That is, "I" descends into the arena of human activity only to highlight what is wrong with others rather than with itself: "Let us be content with a little. . . . In that way I avoid . . ." (IX, 51). "I" participates in failure or human weakness only as part of "we" or the even more ambiguous "one"; the very fact of discerning and saying "we" is a step toward disengagement of the speaker's responsibility. "If I spend two nights in the town I am like its inhabitants . . ." (V, 49). Within the context of communication established by the rhetorical situation, "I" is the guarantor of what ought to be.

"You" enjoys no such privilege. In the few cases where the pronoun refers directly to "I's" audience, it is an object of instruction, and the use of imperatives is significant: "You should let the stranger speak . . . (V, 14); do not probe too deeply . . . (VI, 25); look in his eyes . . . (VIII, 50). Far more frequent, however, is an implicit assimilation or at least association of "I's" audience to mankind as public: the sycophants and the intruded-upon, the predisposed and undiscerning who share equal responsibility for the lamentable state of affairs which prevails. "People tolerate chiromancers and divines who . . . deceive very easily those who seek to be deceived" (XIV, 69). It is up to the listeners to decide whether the shoe fits.[7]

Finally, there are the numerous instances of apostrophe: "I" addresses directly a "you" which is singular but not individualized, since it is either an anonymous voice in a dialogue or a type identified by an initial or a borrowed name. Just as "I" is a refraction of La Bruyère, "you" is an oblique representation of his contemporaries, and the same tunnel vision is at work since the reader could always apply the critical example to his neighbor rather than himself. "Gold glitters, you [vous] tell me, on Philémon's clothes . . . You [tu] are mistaken, Philémon . . ." (V, 27). Witness as well the extraordinary popularity of the keys to the *Characters*. (Santeul, who was reportedly happy and flattered with his character portrait (XII, 56), is the exception to the rule.)

Vision in the *Characters* is a function of the extensive

nature of *caractère*, the variety and interaction of social types, and on another level the discontinuous presentation of the work. The result is a vision in motion, playing over the range of human activity, highlighting certain aspects and imposing finally its own particular elucidation. Observation of significant detail creates a *caractère* which is perceived to be in a kind of perpetual generation, expressed by a syntax of potential, but the code is "broken" almost immediately by the author's use of verbs of discovery and revelation, and characterial process is judged to be degenerative through figures of dehumanization (pejorative hyperbole and metaphor).

Just as the figures of theater and foreign land confer on the observer the function of guide and interpreter, the other metaphors provide insight into the process of deterioration which is central to the problem. The ability to use forceful metaphor joins with an oratorical presentation to create a viewpoint of convincing superiority from which to criticize and to judge. It now remains to ascertain what part models, i.e., favorable or positive types, play in a vision of things.

III *Integrity*

Models are in fact the opposite of *caractères*: Their elucidation counteracts the process of depersonalization. Vision not only seeks out the dark corners and backstages which the eccentrics would prefer to hide, but illuminates as well the positive side of behavior, even if it be only a possibility rather than a reality. "People speak so much ill of that man, and I see so little, that I begin to suspect he has an unwelcome merit which eclipses that of others" (VIII, 39). We have already seen *caractères* in tandem and a predilection for two-part composition. In the case of models, this juxtaposition creates a definite impression of a negative/positive opposition, especially since favorable cases are only rarely presented in isolation (VII, 22; XII, 28, 66).[8]

Just as direct address of one's public is a corrective to the falseness of speech as currently practiced, the men of personal merit (II) are in diametrical opposition to the usurpers of wealth (VI). Another case in point is the use of the word *peuple*. Ambiguous even today, in the *Characters* it may refer to people, political subjects, or simply "others." (The element common to all instances is the notion of "those below oneself.") The author takes advantage of the ambiguity to highlight the flux of a social situation, but uses it *against* the transgressors rather than *for* the victims. *Peuple* in the sense of the lower classes has no chapter in the book, but is nevertheless represented in a number of contexts. On the other hand, its ethical status is essentially based in rhetoric rather than political or social reformism. The same is true of the poor (VI, 44, 49) and the famous remark on the peasants (XI, 128):

[*Peuple*] means more than one thing. . . . There is the common people as opposed to the great: that is the populace, the mob; and there is the people as opposed to the wise, able, and virtuous men: that is the great as well as the small. (IX, 53).

If the notion is not completely independent of society, it is nevertheless obliquely related to the traditional social hierarchy rather than an integral part of it.[9]

A large number of remarks conclude with a twist, a shift from negative to positive: from appearances to the "real" explanation, as we saw in the previous chapter, but also from a behavioral to a moral plane. Models are reversed images of human failings, but they belong as well to a different order of things: "The contrary of rumor . . . is often the truth (XII, 38; VIII, 40); A very wealthy man . . . but to live happily is perhaps the privilege of others (VI, 1); I see a man . . . I should like to see . . ." (VIII, 31; IX, 2).[10] Comparison to Pascal's "reversal of extremes" (*renversement du pour au contre*, Br. 328; Laf. 183) is particularly enlightening:

> If he boasts, I humiliate him
> If he humbles himself, I raise him up
> And contradict him always
> Until he understands
> That he is an incomprehensible monster
> (Br. 420; Laf. 245)

Where the author of the *Pensées* was seeking systematically to readjust man's distorted and one-sided image of himself, La Bruyère moves in one direction only, away from what he sees as excess and presumption. His ideal is a kind of "integrity," of which the textual components are simplicity, congruence, and a harmony to be found in the past.

Like "I" and "you," the models in the *Characters* appear in a variety of types and classes: from Socrates (II, 34; XII, 66), Condé (II, 32), and Bishop Fénelon (XV, 30), to the great king (X, 35) or the citizen (IX, 24). More contemporary social figures are the so-called men of wit, intelligence and quality, and the *honnête homme*, whom La Bruyère praises but sees as subordinate to men of goodness, wisdom, and merit (XII, 55; II, 30; IX, 12). "I can only conclude that greatness and discernment are two different things, and that love of virtue and the virtuous is yet a third" (IX, 13). To see what makes them models, however, we need to examine them structurally and functionally rather than nominatively, since their "model" status is a result of the integrity just mentioned.[11]

In opposition to the characters who accumulate and show off in the hope of distinguishing themselves, are those whose modesty and simplicity confer on them a kind of second-degree distinction, in reaction to such egregious self-importance. Various terms express what is at bottom an ethic of moderation, generosity, and humility. Literature should be "simple" and "natural" (I, 17, 44, 50, 54), for avoidance of the Gothic and barbaric (I, 15, 38) is the best route to the sublime (I, 55, cf. 30). This is equally true of sacred eloquence, whose efficacy is a function of its simplicity (XIII, 26; XV; XVI, 22). In the social realm, affected speech (V) is as pernicious and no more welcome than the excessive makeup which hides women's natural beauty (III).

A beautiful woman is charming in her naturalness; she loses nothing for being in casual dress and with no other adornment than that which she derives from her beauty and her youth. . . . In the same way a good man is respected for himself, independently of all the outward signs which he might affect to make his person more solemn or his virtue more apparent. (XII, 29).

On a more ethical and metaphysical level, simplicity is the ability to accept oneself as one is, to be content with quality and virtue for their own sakes, nothing more and nothing less (VIII, 31; XI, 71; XII, 109). Chapter II in particular contains several theoretical remarks on the discretion, abnegation, and obscurity

Vision

which are the marks of merit, including a veritable
sermon on self-reliance (11). [12]

In a similar spirit, congruence (my term) is the
recognition of propriety and proportion, the acknowledg-
ment of an order in things which should be respected.
It is of course particularly necessary in literary efforts,
not a surprising position for a man of La Bruyére's
time, whether applied to style, character, or critical
judgment (I). It is also the foundation, or should be,
of the relationship between subject and ruler (X, 1, 27,
28), and more generally represents a healthy reciprocity
in opposition to the mutual jealousies of society (V, 32,
53). But as a quasi-aesthetic notion of the integrity of
the whole—"beautiful things are less so when out of
place" (XIV, 18)—it applies to all sectors.

How many men resemble those trees already grown strong
which are transplanted into gardens, where they surprise
those who see them in lovely places where they were never
seen growing . . . (VI, 22); They say gambling is the social
equalizer; but conditions are so strangely disproportionate
and there is so deep and great a gap between one rank and
another, that it hurts one's eyes to see such extremities come
together; it is like discordant music, like colors that clash,
words that fall harshly on the ear or noises and sounds that
make one shudder; in a word, it is the reversal of all propriety (VI, 71); A man subject to prejudice, if he dares
accept a secular or ecclesiastical honor, is a blind man who
seeks to paint, a mute responsible for a speech or a deaf
man criticizing a symphony (XII, 41).

Images like the tiler tiling (II, 16), Mignard is Mignard
(II, 24), Mercury is Mercury (XII, 21); and definitions
of the good man as one who does good (II, 44) or the
rich man taking in more than he spends (VI, 49) seem
redundant until we recall that a man at court no longer

[79]

calls things by their names (VIII, 62; V, 6, 23, 69).
Likewise, one should adapt one's talents to proper
goals (II, 26; XII, 68, 81); and compared to a charlatan,
a doctor whose remedies fit the illness is a welcome
figure (XIV, 66, 68). Wise men are equally praise-
worthy for their good fortune and their good conduct
(XII, 74), and omitting the fact that Socrates danced
is proof of a petty turn of mind (II, 34).

Socrates is also cited (XII, 56) for having depicted
human faults and weaknesses "naturally," i.e., accurately
and realistically. He is thus doubly exemplary: His
detractors, again, are incapable of appreciating his
talents, but second and more important, he belongs to
an antiquity which is the locus of an ideal, a solidity
and a perfection from which we have fallen away. This
is of course the position of an Ancient, but it is not
simply a literary view: The Roman was both courageous
and learned (II, 29), and Rome is proposed at some
length as the epitome of taste, discretion, and a sense
of proportion in all things (VII, 22). The pleasures and
refinements of earlier times have disappeared (XI, 118;
XIII, 10; XIV, 34), and we are left with an abominable
situation. "The civility, consideration and courtesy of
elderly people of both sexes make me think highly of
the so-called old days" (XII, 83). Whether it be in
regard to women's affectation (III, 6), overnight prestige (VIII, 32, 57; XII, 59), a courtier turned pious
(XIII, 18), a commoner rehabilitated (XIV, 3), or
sacred eloquence as entertainment (XV, 1), the passage
of time is the context and symbol of a general degrada-
tion, most often expressed by the notion of *becoming*.
(La Bruyère's frequent use of the present perfect to
express the results of a pernicious process of change,
e.g., (VI), is fundamentally different from the "eternal

present" with which Pascal and La Rochefoucauld
define mankind's inconsistency, and from the succession
of presents which Montaigne sees as distinct but equally
valid and worthy of recording.)

In a few cases, time appears to be on the side of the
moraliste (V, 36; IX, 17; XII, 25), and some remarks
deal with improvement in the future, but that improvement is usually called for, not to say hoped for, rather
than assured (II, 10; VIII, 44; XI, 46; XII, 107). Indeed,
for every such reference one could find one or two others
which advocate a resistance to Fashion (XIII) and
Custom (XIV), a divesting or a retreat from a struggle
which is lost (II, 43; VI, 47; IX, 25). Like *peuple*, the
future in the *Characters* has essentially a rhetorical
value, in opposition to an undesirable present, and in
that sense it is also a kind of refuge. The most striking
examples occur in the portrait of the parvenus, which
is also the most realistically and historically situated of
all the chapters. The author "kills off" a number of
characters through a kind of poetic justice (VI, 17, 40,
70), and cites poverty here and now as probable proof
of happiness in the next life (VI, 26).

One must admit it, the present is for the rich, the future for
the good and the capable. Homer survives and always will
. . . were there tax-farmers in ancient Greece? what has become of the presumptuous people who despised Homer?
(VI, 56; VIII, 95).

For typology, for social and temporal relationships,
and for the tone in which they are expressed, no passage
is closer to the vital center of the *Characters*. As typified
by the presence of tax-farmers and financiers, the world
is in dislocation, out of joint. Everywhere are images of
excess, disproportion, and deterioration. Almost by

definition, change appears unhealthy, uncontrolled and, above all, unwelcome. Given the rhetorical situation of the work, and a certain "moral" content, it would seem that La Bruyère not only borrows the themes and criticisms of contemporary preachers, as documented by Lange and Jasinski, but is to a great extent tempted to reproduce the performance and experience of pulpit oratory as well. "What will become of these fashions when time itself shall have disappeared? Virtue alone, so little in fashion, is beyond the reach of time" (XIII, 31).

Virtue in the *Characters*, however, refers essentially to personal worth rather than Christian morality. "The only others comparable to Saint Augustine are Plato and Cicero" (XVI, 31). Outside specifically religious contexts (XIII, 27; XV, 30; XVI) it is only rarely defined in terms of a divine investiture or respect of divine precepts (III, 4; V, 20). [13] Integrity (the critical and structural equivalent of virtue) exists by definition at the beginning of the socio-ethical process rather than at its completion. Virtue conquers the passage of time by never really being subjected to it, and could usually be defined as what those who are under scrutiny do not possess for having lost, forgotten, or cast it aside. This definition by reaction is fundamental to La Bruyère's vision of self-in-society, and it is not a mere play on words to call that vision *reactionary*. His criticism of the present in very concrete terms distinguishes him from La Rochefoucauld and all but a small part of Pascal, but the resemblance to certain reformist texts of the eighteenth century stems from a similar field of inquiry rather than a common ethic. One could also cite his approval of the Revocation of the Edict of Nantes (X, 35), his attitude toward William of Orange (XII,

119), and his reference to God as guarantor of order through a certain amount of inequality (XVI, 49).

The term *reactionary* should not, however, be considered pejorative or ideological censure. It is certainly true that the *status quo ante* is not subjected to the same scrutiny which La Bruyère applies to the present, but readers are more interested in what he did and how, than in what he might have done, i.e., did not do. Furthermore, we are the richer that he should have dwelt so successfully on the negative examples which have, as a result, come to be the texts for which he is remembered: the *Characters* is the work of a writer whose positive ethical ideal is presented as an aesthetic of the negative.[14]

Thus, La Bruyère's fascination with the figure of the religious hypocrite (*faux dévot*), and in particular his lengthy rebuttal of Tartuffe (XIII, 24), can almost certainly be attributed to the importance of *code*. Onuphre is a spectacular and unique example of a character who has mastered the system, thanks to a "perfect but false imitation of piety," and whose *caractère* is a juxtaposition of successes. Ménalque (XI, 7) is at the other extreme, hopelessly and no less spectacularly awash in a sea of signs. In an oblique relationship to the Ménalque/Onuphre continuum of social presence, is the man whose honorable qualities are summed up in his unfamiliarity with the Court (VIII, 1). All three obviously belong to the author's work, but as I am using the terms the first two belong primarily to *aesthetic*, the third to *ethic*. The eccentrics are an ironic tribute to the center, and that part "outside ourselves" (XI, 76), the "something for which to reproach oneself" (XI, 136), is mankind's misfortune but the reader's gain.

La Bruyère plays on the contradiction between social and ethical distinction in his remark on insipid character (V, 1), and he must have sensed the greater inherent interest of tension and detail over a static and abstract integrity. Virtue as its own excuse is more important, perhaps, but less colorful and dynamic than the significant disproportion of a coquette who dresses up as she passes away (III, 7), Sannion the hunter if only he could shoot straight (VII, 10), or Iphis whose foot keeps him home (XIII, 14). In La Bruyère's hands, that misdirected consistency, the logical result of a certain human weakness or negative potential, culminates in a disproportion which is not only a "sign" of the times but one which still signifies in a very modern way. "The endearments of the great . . . complete his downfall; he is dazed and bewildered, in a state of alienation" (IX, 50).[15]

CHAPTER 6

Appendix I: The Characters, *1688-96*

Chap.	Ed. I-III 1688	IV 1689	V 1690	VI 1691	VII 1692	VII-IX 1694-96
I	35	51	61	64	67	69
II	23	31	37	39	42	44
III	37	55	65	66	81	81
IV	18	67	79	81	86	85
V	35	58	77	77	80	83
VI	29	46	68	75	79	83
VII	4	13	19	19	19	22
VIII	39	63	76	87	96	101
IX	19	37	44	55	57	56
X	10	19	22	23	32	34
XI	73	122	139	146	152	159
XII	30	85	99	106	110	119
XIII	10	17	18	29	29	31
XIV	18	46	58	68	69	73
XV	15	22	24	25	28	30
XVI	24	31	36	36	45	49
Epilogue	1	1	1	1	1	1

CHAPTER 7

The Dialogues on Quietism

THE *Dialogues* were published posthumously by a
certain Abbé Dupin in 1699, and there remains
considerable doubt whether the complete text is by
La Bruyère. He probably wrote most of them, while
his editor subsequently saw fit to make sizable corrections and additions to the manuscript.

Quietism was the religious doctrine according to
which the soul, in order to find God, must remain in a
state of complete inactivity and passive (quiet) con-
templation of the divine, suppressing human initiative
and submitting totally to divine will. The term was
used in the seventeenth century to designate the doctrine
of a Spanish priest, Miguel de Molinos, who held that
even a wish to act—whether for good or ill—was an
offense in God's sight, and that in any case one's actions
only involved man's lower, baser aspects. Condemned by
Rome, he died in prison in 1696. In France, a form
known as semiquietism was advocated by Madame
Guyon and Archbishop Fénelon, the latter in his *Explication des maximes des saints sur la vie intérieure
(Explication of the Maxims of the Saints on the Inner
Life)*, 1697. Violently opposed by Bishop Bossuet, he
appealed his case to Rome which, after considerable
political pressure by Louis XIV acting at Bossuet's
instigation, condemned Fénelon's work in 1699. The

The Dialogues on Quietism

Archbishop submitted completely to Rome's decision. La Bruyère's nine dialogues deal with the role of prayer; divine omnipresence; activity seen as a source of evil by the quietists; sainthood and soul-searching as opposed to quietist practice; quietist indifference as unchristian; quietist abandonment of Scripture and Christ the Mediator; the pernicious effects of beatitude and "essential union" with the divine; love and charity excluded from the quietist essence of God; and the notion of evil as absent from quietist prayer and beatitude.

These religious and spiritual matters are presented in discussions between a young woman known as "the pentitent" and her spiritual director. This is perhaps the only obvious link with the *Characters,* in their condemnation of fashionable religious practices in general and spiritual directors in particular, but there are other literary reminiscences as well. In the first dialogue, it is made clear that the director is drawing the penitent away from her family, who are more orthodox in their beliefs, a situation which recalls Molière's *Tartuffe* although it is not developed at all. The resemblance is enhanced somewhat by the dialogue, which by the end of the century was being used to present relatively abstruse material or new knowledge, as in Fontenelle's *Entretiens sur la pluralité des mondes* (*Conversations on the World and the Universe*), 1686. The major predecessor, however, one whose influence is felt on every page, is Pascal's *Lettres de Louis de Montalte à un Provincial de ses amis* (*Letters from Louis de Montalte to a Friend in the Provinces*), 1656–57. A minor masterpiece too little known by nonspecialists, Pascal's work purported to be a series of eighteen letters written by Montalte to keep his friend abreast of recent develop-

ments in religious thinking. In fact, they are a defense
of Jansenist writings via a lively, witty, and ironic
debunking of Jesuit doctrine, which Pascal effects by
having Montalte seek enlightenment from a number
of Jesuit representatives who reveal only their own
fatuous bad faith and thereby contaminate and dis-
credit the doctrine they would uphold.

Alas, La Bruyère is no second Pascal. The prose is
dry, abstract, and theoretical rather than an emanation
of human concern, a religious discussion rather than
a courtroom testing of discourse. One of the problems
seems to be that, compared to the rhetorical situation
of the *Letters*, the penitent, whose ingenuousness is
sincere, plays only the role of a *confident* as opposed
to Montalte's masterfully hypocritical reporter. Nor does
the addition of the penitent's learned doctor brother
(VI) or the gentleman (IX) alleviate the impression of
pedestrian and stuffy treatment of the issues at stake.

To be sure, the text has its moments. The penitent's
innocent-mindedness sometimes reveals contradictions
in the director's statements, and he is occasionally
drawn into some unfortunate (for him) formulations
and overstatements:

Did [Saint Theresa] have, like us, an infallible method . . .
invariable rules by which to elevate persons of both sexes, a
child, a valet, a peasant, a mason, to the sublimity of inef-
fable prayer (II); In the first place, Sir, we do not love
God, and I'll thank you to remember it . . . (VII).

And like Agnes compared to Arnophe in Molière's
L'Ecole des femmes (*School for Wives*), 1662, the
penitent is the best evidence of the totalitarian and
almost blasphemous pretentions of the director:

Penitent: I tried to become like a statue or a tree stump . . .
Director: I once knew a girl of eighteen . . . at present, I
wish you could see her. She has become a stump, a timber,
so much deadwood [*un corps mort*]; she is so emptied of
mind and spirit, she has been so accustomed to doing no
thinking any longer, that you would think she had lost her
power to reason. (II)
Penitent: Our Father, who art no more in heaven than on
earth or in hell, who art everywhere present, I neither wish
nor desire that hallowed be thy name. . . . (V)

Finally, there are a few points where a character
reaches enough intensity of feeling to become truly
eloquent:

Doctor: But sister, can you really say that he is following his
own will? that he is acting by propriety and activity [tech-
nical terms]? that these are human actions, actions of Adam,
sins which must be confessed?
Penitent: Dear brother . . . if only you knew, if you could
feel but once what it is to be an ardent soul . . . if you could
know the pleasure of renouncing one's own activity, of im-
mersing oneself in the sea of divine will: what peace, what
repose, what glowing nights for that soul. . . . (IV).

On the whole, however, La Bruyère's text manages
neither the sustained majesty of Bossuet's best writing
nor the crafty but engaging innuendo of Pascal's
persona. The *Dialogues* are in a sense a counterexample
of his success in the *Characters*: The earlier writing
elaborated an aesthetic so adequate to the ethical
content as to embody it and perhaps even determine it
to some extent, but La Bruyère seems more at home
with caricature based on observation and judgment than
with quasi-dramatic portrayal of character from within.
In the *Dialogues* his technical skill was simply overbur-
dened by the demands he chose to make on it.

CHAPTER 8

Affinities

THE popularity of the *Characters* continued during the century following their publication, as they went through more than thirty editions. At the same time, of course, other related but original works were being written, and it is the latter that I should like to look at in this chapter. Because the cases of "certifiable" influence are relatively rare, it seems more appropriate to attempt a suggestive trajectory of the *caractère* impulse than to document rather flatly instances of textual borrowings and specific mentions of La Bruyère. I have already tried to show how he fits into his time, and I hope now to show why he is still worth reading and why in fact he still is read. It should be obvious, however, that while La Bruyère's originality can be demonstrated, nevertheless, like all figures in a given tradition, he can legitimately be seen as "transitional" in the sense that he is neither the first nor the last.[1]

I   A First Generation

The *Characters* were imitated almost immediately, and often in an attempt to capitalize on their success. In the first thirty-odd years of the eighteenth century, however, other writers brought something of themselves to the same undertaking and in that sense were, in a way, more faithful to La Bruyère's creative impulse.

Of these, the Duc de Saint-Simon is the only one who deals with the same period of the seventeenth century, although his voluminous memoirs cover the period from 1691 to 1723. Moreover, it is crucial to note that he wrote primarily for himself and is a much better example of literary therapy—not to say vengeance—than La Bruyère. The difference for the modern reader lies essentially in Saint-Simon's no-holds-barred technique: Critical detail and condemnation carry even more weight than in the *Characters* because Saint-Simon wrote about individuals rather than types. It is not completely clear, for example, to what extent Louis XIV is cause and/or effect in La Bruyère's idealization of the sovereign. Saint-Simon's treatment is more specific and more biographical, but he also seems consistently to give with one hand and then take away with the other. "Louis was born good and just . . . The source of the problems lay elsewhere" he says, but he has just noted that "the King's intelligence was less than average" (IV, 950).[2] To add that it was capable of improvement is simply to damn with faint praise, and in any case hardly enough to counterbalance Saint-Simon's indictments of the King's egotism and thirst for glory as exemplified by military campaigns and the palace at Versailles (IV, 1005–7, 1045–47). The royal family also gets highly equivocal treatment, but rather like La Bruyère Saint-Simon is most remembered for his portraits of the hangers-on and intermediaries. His description of the reactions to the news of the Grand Dauphin's death in 1711 is generally considered his masterpiece. It is reminiscent of La Bruyère in that the whole situation is presented as an occasion for reconnaissance and discovery: "All those present were most expressive participants; one's own eyes, with no prior familiarity with the court, were enough to discern the self-interest painted on their faces ..." (III, 815–25). Indeed, like many works before it and the *Characters* in particular, the whole work is full of references to seeing, masks, discovery, etc.[3]

Where it differs is first of all in the use of unflattering and often intimate physical detail which can be said to carry La Bruyère's technique to its logical conclusion, but which has no real equivalent in the earlier writer. Gnathon (XI, 121), whose shocking table manners are one extreme in the *Characters*, would be only average in a set of memoirs where the writer has no qualms about literary or linguistic niceties and does a portrait of the Regent, describing the latter on his toilet (VII, 344–45).[4] The other major difference is far greater range and flexibility in the point of view. The same semiological function is at work, but because he is writing a chronicle Saint-Simon has much greater recourse to scene and narration, and in fact his panoramic description of the mourners and rejoicers at the Grand Dauphin's death is one of the most cinematographic in French literature. In varying degrees these two points— the presentation of physical or "realistic" detail, and the interplay of character and narrative—seem to be the major elements in the definition and evolution of the *caractère* tradition.

Novels like Lesage's *Diable boiteux* (*The Devil on Two Sticks*), 1707, and *Gil Blas de Santillane* (1715–35) present a daily-life atmosphere which with a few exceptions had previously been reserved for the rarefied world of the Court. In the earlier work Asmodée, in order to entertain Don Cléophas Zambullo for letting him out of the bottle in which he was imprisoned, lifts the roofs off houses in Madrid so that Don Cléophas, like the reader, can see what is going on inside. In *Gil Blas*,

Lesage uses the picaresque form to parade a series of social types and characters in both the Spanish and French traditions. The plot line is a pretext for stringing together sketches and vignettes, and the narrator is decidedly two-dimensional compared to what he will become later in the century. Nonetheless, there is already a distinction to be made vis-à-vis La Bruyère: When a character actually appears in the novel, whether or not he is also described, he rarely fits the *caractère* mold. That is, the foreshortening and condensation of a series of repetitious traits or actions which constitute a *caractère* are now found solely in description; when a character appears the scene is much more akin to a once-only theatrical scene, or anticipates the more rounded existence of future novelistic characters. It is the difference between the segment of *Gil Blas* (II) devoted to Doctor Sangrado, a quack, and a passing reference to the licentiate Campanario, "whom you hear even before he appears. He begins talking as he comes in off the street and keeps on until he's left again. . . . Not only is he a merciless talker, but he never stops repeating himself" (VIII).

The point is not just that Campanario is reminiscent of Théodecte (V, 12) in his particular foible, but that within the novel he has only a second-hand existence and is therefore much more a synthesis than an illustration. At the other extreme is Lesage's *Turcaret* (1709), a comedy in which Monsieur Turcaret, suitor to a baroness, is exposed as a tax-farmer and usurer, and in which at the same time an unscrupulous Chevalier, hoping to cash in on others' naïveté, is in fact duped by his own valet. The play recalls seventeenth-century comedy with its parvenu protagonist and "just deserts" resolution. At the same time, it is more a comedy of manners than of character, since Turcaret is not just an eccentric and a fool, but a dangerous one as well. The banter still feeds on stereotypes of class and category, but Lesage's tone is ambiguous and often grating: There is no doubt that for him the comic conflict has a social and economic content, and expresses a real tension in contemporary *mores*. In that respect, the play's predecessors are not so much *The Miser* or *The Would-be Gentleman* as a whole body of antifinancier literature of which La Bruyère's (VI) is the best-known example. Still, what distinguishes the work from La Bruyère's is greater use of financial terms, but even more important a dramatic presentation which allows us to follow a single instance from close up, rather than a far-off and consequently foreshortened view of a financier's career. (Périandre (VI, 21) is halfway between trait and narrative.) The technical function of the anecdote is thus as story rather than as one trait in a listing of equivalent characteristics.

Montesquieu's formula for integrating short passages of social observation into a continuous movement was the epistolary novel. If his *Persian Letters* (1721) was not the first example of the genre, it nonetheless represents a major success at an early stage in the development of narrative. Critics are still debating over the unifying "secret chain" which he claimed for it later in his career, but there is little doubt that the novelistic aspect is more fully worked out. Rica and Usbek convey to one another their impressions of Paris, which divides the narrative responsibility, but the author takes pains to characterize both the correspondents through theme and tone. Rica is lighthearted and curious, given to quick and often flippant sketches of the Paris scene, while Usbek is stolid and reflective, tempted more by the essay than the vignette. Into this framework, Montesquieu worked over 150 "selections" averaging between one and two pages in length and dealing with a variety of social, political, and moral issues. There were historical precedents in the visits of foreign dignitaries to Paris, and French accounts of travel to the Middle East; literarily there was Marana's *Espion turc* (*Turkish Spy*) 1684, among others, not to mention the relativistic theme of the foreign point of view to which Montaigne had alluded frequently. La Bruyère made use of the same device, but a number of other letters are also quite similar to his approach. No. 72 on the "decisionary" is probably a direct imitation of Arrias (V, 9), and No. 74 on the Great could come verbatim from the *Characters*. (See as well 48 on the tax-farmer, 52 on women, 56 on gambling, 98 on the vicissitudes of fortune, 99 on the whims of fashion, 124 on the scandal of courtiers, and 130 on the newsmongers.)

On the other hand, Montesquieu's book is clearly of a later period. A certain social decadence is seen as encroaching still further; the religious policies of Louis XIV are roundly criticized and even the Papacy treated in secular fashion; most of all, the theme of the harem as story line gives a palpable and vital shape to the work as compared to the *Characters*. The explicit content and the technique of many of the letters remind one of La Bruyère, but the movement of the whole is quite different. Indeed, Montesquieu takes two large steps toward the novel in that the observations are wrought by a character in the work rather than an implicit orator-*moraliste*, and secondly, because, in the case of Usbek, the author undermines his trustworthiness as philosopher-narrator by tracing the decline and ultimate fall of the harem as a system for whose function Usbek is responsible. Formally and thematically the novel can be considered, among other things, as a bridge between the lively but truncated genre of the *caractère* and two important moments in the history of the French novel, Rousseau's *Julie* (1761) and Laclos' *Liaisons dangereuses* (*Dangerous Acquaintances*), 1784.

Somewhat the same literary situation had prevailed a few years earlier in England, where the *Characters* was translated as early as 1699. How much of the *Tatler* (1700–11) and the *Spectator* (1712–15) was a result of La Bruyère's influence, or the English character tradition, or even other sources like Montaigne and Bacon, has never been satisfactorily sorted out. We do know that Addison and Steele were familiar with the *Characters* and it is not difficult to find close parallels. Not only is La Bruyère mentioned (*Tatler*, 9, 57) and referred to indirectly (*Tatler*, 52; *Spectator*, 45, 564); number 77 of the *Spectator* relies heavily on Ménalque (XI, 7), hardly surprising since it was contributed by Eustace Budgell, the first translator of the French original. Moreover, despite a greater preference for the illustrative anecdote and the chance encounter, some of the most successful English creations recall La Bruyère's: the newsmonger and the pedant (*Tatler*, 155, 158), a string of familiar types (*Spectator*, 148, 151, 152, 156), and, of course, the group portrait of Sir Roger de Coverly and his friends (*Spectator*, 2). On the whole, however, the English writers aimed at a much more explicit and class-oriented goal of adequate social performance, with an optimistic view of installing the bourgeois solidly but graciously, as compared to what La Bruyère often seems to consider a last-ditch ethical stand.[5] To be sure, the stance of the reformist-observer is there, the "Spectator of Manners [rather than] one of the Species" (*Spectator*, 1). Mr. Spectator is sometimes a rather dour onlooker, but thanks to the informal and conversational tone of Addison's contributions, a narrative persona like Isaac Bickerstaff, Esq., and a figure like Roger de Coverly, both carried over from one number to another and for whom there is no real formal equivalent in the *Characters*, the *Tatler* and *Spectator* seem with hindsight to have been moving from a kind of literary journalism toward a new heyday for the essay and toward the narrative forms which were developed at length only a few years later by Fielding and others.[6]

Marivaux was in turn influenced by Addison and Steele, and published a *Spectateur Français* (*French Spectator*) between 1721 and 1724. He is better known for his plays about love and pride, but in his other works there are many traces of the *caractère* tradition. The portrayal of the hypocrite Climal and Marianne, the born coquette, who gives her name to one of Marivaux's novels (1731–42), are too narrative really to be considered *caractères*, and other shorter portraits belong more to the older *précieux* genre. His periodical writings, on the other hand, are full of both portraits and *caractères*. The editor of his *Lettre sur les habitants de Paris* (*Letter on the Inhabitants of Paris*), 1717, even calls him the modern Theophrastus, although he preferred his own signature. The presentation of the latter works also seems contingent and even whimsical: Some sheets contain several bits and anecdotes, while elsewhere a single sequence takes several sheets to complete. One source of unity in Marivaux is his constant preoccupation not only with coquetry, but in general with the problems of self-consciousness and the presentation of self. Unlike La Bruyère, Marivaux is not content to describe and to judge: He seems fascinated as much by the process as by the result. The plays are in a sense the elaboration and testing of a new personality under the stress of love, and Marianne is perplexed by a personal quality and dignity which her surroundings as an orphan belie.[7] In that sense, Marivaux belongs to a tradition of *moraliste* inquiry into being and seeming, is one of the first writers consistently to undertake such inquiry in French narrative literature, and to that extent belongs secondarily and only sporadically to the literary history of the *caractère*. (It is also quite probable that Marivaux had an influence on the developing English novel, along with other French novelists like Lesage and Prévost.)

At one or two points in his periodical writing, his remarks shed considerable light on the evolution of both traditions. In the *Spectateur*, Sheet 1, the narrator tells about having returned to recover a glove at the home of a woman to whom he was greatly attached, and discovering her trying out her simple and naïve airs before a mirror. In its curious pre-Stendhal way, this is another example of the mask image so prevalent in earlier literature. What makes it interesting to readers of La Bruyère is a farreaching change he rings on it in the *Cabinet du philosophe* (*The Philosopher's Study*), 1734. In the lengthy section called "Travels to the True World" (Sheets 6–11), he describes his visit to a world identical to our own, except that there people are naïvely authentic and communicate only what they truly think and feel. One of the fundamental links between La Bruyère and subsequent writers, one which expresses an affinity even where narrative "dilutes" and then absorbs *caractère*, is the notion which I described in relation to the *Characters* as negative/positive. The link is particularly noticeable in works where the function of observer or spectator is important, and Marivaux gives the *moraliste* dichotomy between appearance and reality a curious fillip by emphasizing the true (cf. La Bruyère, who vastly prefers negative illustrations). In *L'Indigent Philosophe* (*The Philosophical Bum*), 1727, the negative/positive distinction expresses a reversal of the traditional social hierarchy so that lower is better, or at least a better place from which to observe. "Of all the theaters in the world, Paris is the one with the best comedy, or the best farce if you will; farce above and farce below" (Sheet 5). This is not only reminiscent of La Bruyère's "populist" stance (VI, 47; IX, 25); it is also a sign that literature will be increasingly, significantly, and even voluntarily situated at lower social levels than the arbiters of seventeenth-century taste would have imagined or accepted. Despite the reactionary philosophy behind it, La Bruyère's depiction of a concrete and current social world was an innovation in the "serious" literature of his time.

The fact that Rameau's nephew (Diderot: *Le Neveu de Rameau*, 1761–74) reads Theophrastus, La Bruyère, and Molière to find out "what to do and what not to say," i.e., how to fool others, is a tribute to the aesthetic staying power of the earlier works as well as an exploitation. Indeed, in its awareness of negative and positive, its obsession with models, copies and eccentrics (*originaux*), and its frequent recourse to animal imagery, Diderot's work is very much in the spirit of its predecessor.

II Caractère *and Narrative*

Typologies of social behavior were one of the literary vogues between approximately 1820 and 1840. Variously called "arts," "codes" and "physiologies," they derived from the increasing volume of medico-philosophical speculation on the relationship between psychology and physiology, and the study of man's character through his features. The tone of such adaptations was less serious than their models (see in particular Lavater's *Physiognomy* and Gall's phrenology), although in the foreword to his *Comédie humaine* (1842) Balzac was obviously intent on the possibility of breaking down his field of inquiry into types, professions, classes, etc., and establishing a comparison between "humanity and animality" by analogy with zoology and other developing sciences.[8] Any reader of Balzac is familiar with his extraordinary capacity to draw characters larger than life and to set them in significant contexts. (The boardinghouse in *Père Goriot* is probably the most famous example.) Two of his earlier works, however, are less well known but curiously close to the *caractère* tradition: the *Code des honnêtes gens* (*Code of Honorable People*), published anonymously in 1824, and the *Physiologie du Mariage* (1829). Pastiches of the Napoleonic civil code and Savarin's *Physiology of Taste* respectively, both works purport to set out for their readers the basic principles and conventions of the society of their time.

The title of the Code is a play on *honnêtes gens* (honest/respectable), an ambiguity left over from earlier times; while the subtitle, "the art of not being the victim of swindlers," is reminiscent of, but seemingly opposed to, the outlook of Rameau's nephew. The work itself contains several elements which recall La Bruyère's

place in the *caractère* tradition: the isolation and definition of certain social types; the further discernment of a
general social ethos to which these types conform; the
condemnation of this code as harmful; and presentation
from a point of view and in a form—basically what we
would call a treatise—other than poetry, drama, or fiction. There is also a major thematic link with La
Bruyère, which is of course the increasing importance of
money. "Nowadays everything is minted [*monétisé*];
one no longer says: 'So-and-So has been named attorney
general, he will uphold the common good of his prov-
ince . . .' How mistaken: 'He has taken a handsome position . . . worth twenty thousand francs' " (III).

As in the *Characters*, the best one can do is define and
judge, although the battle is a losing one. Thieves are a
class unto themselves, a state within the state (*Prole-
gomena*). They are half-breeds, chameleons, vultures,
wolves who prey only on other species; brokers, "like
reptiles, should be classed according to families and carefully described" (III, 2). Their victims are sheep who
leave a bit of their fleece each time they go by, and the
honest man is invulnerable not for his noble simplicity,
but because he carries nothing on him worth stealing
(I):

The perfect swindler . . . has the clothes, the manners, the
speech of respectability; he infiltrates honorable families in
various forms . . . Some even retire and become respectable
once they are rich . . . In fact, he is born and dies every
twenty-four hours, like the insects which Aristotle describes
. . . (I,2).

Even those classes (doctors, notaries, attorneys, bailiffs,
Normans, Gascons, etc.) whom fate has thrown to the
scoffers "take no offense and do not even try to answer

back, for one can hardly speak with one's mouth full"
(III). In fact, the irony lies elsewhere: as Rameau's
nephew well knew, a full understanding of social convention and function is a great temptation to become
more involved rather than to retreat. The ambivalent
fascination with society of an Alceste, a La Bruyère, a
Saint-Simon, or a Balzac—all of them to some extent
its victims—is in a sense expressed in the dual image of
the secret agents employed by the police: "modern-day
Januses, honest on one side, crooked on the other" (I).

The *Physiology* is a series of thirty "meditations"
devoted to the "Science of marriage" (XXII). Balzac
runs through a series of half-ironic statistics to conclude
that there are some four or five hundred thousand "honest and respectable women" in a country with a total
population of thirty million (II–IV). The figures are of
some interest, and Balzac was closer to modern social
science than was La Bruyère, but there are also many
vestiges of more classical techniques. A number of social,
ethical, and literary types serve as reference points in the
analysis, and the typology is often set up with tongue in
cheek, as in the list of reasons, literally from A to Z,
why men marry (I). There are likewise a great many
figurative references to animals, e.g., "Buffon described
animals masterfully, but the biped called a husband is
something else again" (III). (Two of Balzac's coinages
designate husbands who are "minotaurized," and the
"mousetraps" or stratagems by which unfaithful wives
are to be caught.)

The heterogeneity and inconsistent irony of the
Physiology make generalization difficult, but Balzac
clearly considered the institution of marriage a valid
touchstone for analysis of contemporary society. Marriage is perhaps the comedy of comedies (I), but the

Affinities

numerous references to actors and roles show that its dramatic side belongs to social conflict as well as literary tradition. Similarly, comparisons to money and transactions are reminiscent of the *Characters* but are also very definitely an application to the society of Balzac's time rather than mere appropriation of a figure. Finally, his allusions to the battle of the sexes are reinforced by a number of bold analogies to marriage as political system and slavery which are not unworthy of the most radical feminist irony (although his personal viewpoint is somewhat ambivalent). "A woman is a property acquired by contract, she is chattel, for possession is nine points of the law; strictly speaking, she is but a supplement to man" (XII).

Balzac seems to have been very conscious of the format in which he was writing. The dedication and the introduction contain references to the "you" of his public and the problem of speaking in the first person singular or plural. (Two years later, in his preface to *La Peau de chagin* [*The Ass's Skin*], he felt obliged to discuss the difference between an author and the "I" in a literary work, since the *Physiology* had been "attributed by some to an old doctor, by others to a debauched companion of Madame de Pompadour, or to an inveterate misanthropist.") Again in the introduction, he refers to the seriousness of his subject matter and his choice of anecdotal presentation as the least tedious mode of writing on *mores*. He was obviously being coy about it, and anecdotes are by no means the main form of presentation, but as Maurice Bardèche has pointed out, the *Physiology* is a kind of album in which Balzac could begin to set down character sketches, isolated situations, and in general available materials to be used again in the major novels of the 1830's.[9] What the *Characters* was to the novels of Lesage and Montesquieu, the *Physiology* was to Balzac's later work.

Balzac's only specific reference to La Bruyère (XXV, 1) is a quotation to be refuted, somewhat like the latter on Pascal. The refutation, however, takes the surprising form of a jumble of letters and punctuation run together without forming any recognizable word, and the next remark begins "Up until thirty years of age, a woman's face is a book written in a foreign language . . ." La Bruyère's image of deciphering has been turned around and set in a rather different context. On the other hand, even though Balzac supposedly adapts his techniques from more scientific sources, the results can sometimes be remarkably similar to the *Characters*: "The marital customs inspection [*douane conjugale*] is the rapid but thorough examination of the physical, emotional and mental state of all those who come to visit your wife. . . . The manner in which one approaches your wife, speaks to her, looks at her, takes leave of her. . . . The signs of her own happiness can be found even in the slightest disarray of her hairdo . . ." (XV).

The title and subtitle of *Madame Bovary* (*Provincial Manners*), 1857, closely parallel the personal/social interaction in the *Characters*. Flaubert's greater use of specific and concrete vocabulary—particularly medical terms, but things and objects in general—is a continuation and extension of a certain tradition as well as a break with Romantic practice. Perhaps the most compelling reason for discussing the work here, however, is that it has the breadth of vision of a Balzac, but like La Bruyère in a single book; furthermore, it is written in the narrative mode but offers at the same time an unusual opportunity to study characters at different levels of development.

Emma Bovary, married to a mediocre country doctor, lives out a life of boredom and unfulfilled expectation in the stifling atmosphere of little provincial towns. Her "problem," however, is not only things as they are, but things as she imagines they might be from the Romantic literature of her education (I, 6). Flaubert's criticism is a more sweeping one than La Bruyère's, but not really different in kind: Like countless *caractères*, Emma longs to be what she is not and chases after models which are not only inferior, but irrelevant. His critical vision could even be said to include La Bruyère's own outlook: The past as Emma thinks of it, particularly Madame de la Vallière (I, 6; II, 14), is obviously akin to literary types and just as misleading, and in their mediocrity Flaubert's characters do not even become the "faithful copies" stigmatized by La Bruyère. At the characterial level, however, both authors are dealing with an inner emptiness, which Emma seeks to fill via emulation of literary and historical stereotypes.

Indeed, Flaubert uses many of the techniques we have seen in the *Characters*. Emma's thoughts are compared disparagingly to a greyhound (I, 7) and Rodolphe describes her as "gaping after love like a carp after water on the kitchen table" (II, 7). Equally typical of Flaubert's subtle and so-to-speak disloyal genius is free indirect discourse, of which he is often considered the first major practitioner and which constantly points up the mediocrity of Emma's yearnings: "What sunny days they had had. . . . Any woman who had made so many sacrifices certainly had the right to a few whims" (II, 7). But most reminiscent of earlier French ethical analysis is the lucid scrutiny of the confusion in Emma's mind between being and seeming, and particularly between reality and fiction. Her most notable predecessor is, of course, Don Quixote, but she also exemplifies one of the major strains of the human condition described by the *moralistes*. "In her desire, she confused the sensuous pleasures of living with the joys of the heart. . . . At one and the same time she longed to die and to live in Paris" (I, 9). We see her frequently looking out a window, on a kind of ethical threshold not unlike the doorways through which a La Bruyère *caractère* enters a drawing room. Even her decision to go with Rodolphe on the horseback ride which will lead to her seduction is in fact made for the riding habit (II, 9), a significant disproportion, to say the least.

In the context of the novel, however, this disproportion and her general inability to make distinctions or establish priorities are merely symptoms of an almost pathological confusion which culminates in a veritable flight from life (II, 14) and leads step by step to her suicide. (Cf. the summary and rather rhetorical "executions" administered by La Bruyère.) Emma exists in a narration: Many elements tell one story, whereas in the *caractère* many manifestations are bound together to suggest rather than delineate the (narrative) potential in a single character or character-type. Emma's husband is an excellent example of the latter.

To begin with, his name denotes a placid, bovine temperament confirmed throughout the novel by a general inclination to torpor: "his mind at rest and his flesh at peace, he rode off ruminating his happiness, like those who mull over after dinner the taste of the truffles they are digesting" (I, 5). Metonymic details like his famous cap (I, 1) suggest a general truth beyond their immediate function and context. "His placid back was irritating to look at, and she saw all the platitude of his character spread across his coat. . . . 'Oh,' she said to herself, 'he carries a knife in his pocket like a peasant' " (II, 5). It is this essentialism, the spinning out of a "given," which places Charles squarely in the *caractère* tradition. He is condemned inevitably to express his basic inadequacy in whatever he undertakes or allows himself to be drawn into.

The sum of Charles's existence is exhausted in a series of imperfect tenses; he does what he can but it is never more than a low level of performance, and, worse yet, a repetition and confirmation of his bovinity. "Still half asleep, he let himself be rocked by the peaceful gait of his horse. . . . The flat countryside stretched out as far as the eye could see. . . . From time to time he would open his eyes; then . . . he would soon fall into a kind of doze . . ." (I, 2). Emma, on the other hand, is a creature of conditionals: What could be, ought to be and finally might have been. She is in a sense more Pascalian in her refusal to remain in the present—"she could not imagine that the calm of her present life was the happiness she had dreamed of" (I, 6)—and spends her whole narrative existence hoping for and trying to create an event which Charles is incapable of providing. (Once again, Flaubert goes beyond La Bruyère to mock the misplaced and mediocre *simplicity* of Charles, whose "How pleasant to be home again at last" on their return from the ball (I, 8), is the devastating opposite of Emma's severe letdown.)

Nor are her other encounters any more helpful. Rodolphe strikes cynical poses and affects a manly cigar, but he thinks and speaks in clichés (II, 8, 9, 12). Léon is a mixture of Emma's daydreaming and Charles's passivity (II, 2, 6; III, 4, 5). And Bournisien is basically a peasant in priest's clothing, who like Charles misconstrues a psychological deficiency as a simple physical problem (II, 6).

Madame Bovary is a book about platitude: geographical, physical, and spiritual. A provincial countryside described as the epitome of flatness, immobility, and negation (II, 1) is a larger stage than La Bruyère's but one equally populated by two-dimensional, "flat" characters in both the aesthetic and ethical senses of the word. At the center is Emma, a character whose recognition and refusal of such platitude is failure of yet a different order, a turn of mind which was escapism even before a confrontation ever really occurred. All of the minor characters display a series of traits or activities which may appear sequential at first, but which are quickly revealed to be parallel manifestations of the same inner void, a consistent and repetitive urge to perform inadequate and even ridiculous gestures. There is more texture to Charles's characterization than to Binet's, whose lathe completely expresses the circular, monotonous drone of his personality, but the mechanism and the net result are the same (II, 2). Emma is, so to speak, surrounded by *caractères,* and one of the crowning ironies of the novel is her attempt to trade one set of stereotypes for another.

Her "I have a lover!" (II, 9) is well known, but readers of La Bruyère and Saint-Simon will experience a special pleasure of recognition in the portrait of the old Duc de Laverdière (I, 8). Dribbling sauce down his chin, he is the living rejoinder to Emma's romanticism and nostalgia for a more glorious bygone era. Homais, on the other hand, the pretentious pharmacist who resembles a *caractère* in his slogan-mongering and self-promotion is nevertheless at least as reminiscent of Molière's characters in the sense that he has a "destiny," i.e., he moves through a single action to a new situation. But it is precisely because his rise feeds on the mediocrity of others that he becomes the capstone of the ironic Flaubertian ethic, an indictment of the world, but no less a part of it.

Compared to the oratorical lucidity of the *Characters,* Flaubert's vision is everywhere and nowhere in the novel, an irony present on every page but never quite heavy-handed because it is a complete and almost seamless system. The famous scene of the Agricultural Fair (II, 8), for example, is obvious manipulation on the author's part, yet a careful reading reveals it as the high point of a whole series of animal images throughout the work. In a sense, Flaubert uses both the *caractère* mode and its opposite. The minor characters go nowhere: Charles ends up virtually where he started and literally never even gets off the ground. Emma's life story, on the other hand, is told in great detail, but at the same time subjected to a progressive leveling-down: "She was as disgusted with him as he was tired of her. Emma was rediscovering in adultery all the platitudes of marrage" (III, 6). This foreshortening and flattening-out, already crucial to the definition of *caractère*, is the technique which not only binds together setting, character, and action in the novel, but also reveals them all as identically "flat." The synthesis in *Madame Bovary* is narrative, however, rather than simply characterial, and because it transcends the latter, the work comes to exist as a complete and separate document, a world unto itself rather than a quasi-historical reflection. The author withdraws as far as possible in order that the system appear self-sufficient, and this sense of autonomous function is increasingly important to the evolution of the *caractère* tradition.

The various elements of *caractère* writing may of course go off in different directions. The theme of money, only one spurious fulfillment among others in the *Characters*, became in Lesage and especially in Balzac a major dynamic element and almost a law unto itself. More generally, the inner emptiness which La Bruyère decried took on more and more the trappings of a clinical problem. Balzac's *Pathology of Social Life* attests to both the validity and the enormity of the project, and by the time Zola came to write his *Experimental Novel* (1880) medical science had become such an underpinning that the writer claimed to be dealing with literal lesions in his characters.[10] Here again, *Madame Bovary* seems to contain in suspension the literary history of the medical profession: Charles is the mediocre being who happens to be a doctor and like Canivet is representative of practitioners as pretentious as they are inadequate (Montaigne, II, 37; any number of quacks in Molière; La Bruyère's Carro Carri, XIV, 68; and Doctor Sangrado in *Gil Blas*). On the other hand, insofar as Flaubert is represented in the text, his sardonic Doctor Larivière fulfills that function.

One could also align subsequent "human comedies" and the social realities which they transpose, from Montesquieu and Saint-Simon (the Regency) to Proust's *belle époque*, where Madame Verdurin's salon like La Bruyère's social world (VII, 4) is composed of so many cliques, states within the state. (See also Thackeray's *Book of Snobs*, 1848.) The major French novelists of the nineteenth century extended the literary world to include the provinces, but Dickens' Uriah Heep and Faulkner's Flem Snopes are still as suggestively named as any *caractère*. Somewhat more akin to the techniques of the tradition is Sherwood Anderson's *Winesburg,*

Ohio (1919), a one-volume study of "grotesques," a word La Bruyère uses once (XII, 26), and, like the *Characters*, a gallery of portraits rather than a single narrative, although each portrait is more a short story or tale than the hypothetical events which reveal the *caractères*.

Finally, other authors have preferred to develop animal figurations, whether social, as in Becque's *Les Corbeaux* (*The Vultures*) 1882; symbolic, like Gregor Samsa turned beetle in Kafka's *Metamorphosis* (1915) and Ionesco's rhinoceroses (1960); or zoological, like Desmond Morris' *The Naked Ape* (1967) and various studies on aggression in man.

III *Modernity*

In their most basic definitions, *caractère* and narrative are incompatible, but some modern writers have explicitly turned that incompatibility to advantage. Norman Lear's Archie Bunker is not only a *caractère* in the sense that he can be depended upon to spew out inadequacies, but reminiscent of the Flaubertian situation to the extent that he sees others in turn as *caractères*, foreshortening their humanity and spontaneity into racial and ethnic stereotypes. Moreover, if he were the subject of a single play he would resemble a character out of Molière, but in a weekly television series he encourages and enables us to induce the source of his activity. The same is true of Neil Simon's paradigmatic *Odd Couple* (New York: Random House, 1966), reminiscent of Giton/Phédon in their opposition and their comical negative potential (Oscar is sloppy/ Felix is neat). In *Diary of a Mad Housewife* by Sue Kaufman (New York: Bantam, 1970), Tina is driven to confide her thoughts and her frustrations to her journal, since her husband has totally sur-

[111]

rendered to the social and professional necessity of wearing clothes for their labels, eating the right food, and being seen with the right people: his *caractère* is the starting point for her narrative. (Cf. Emma Bovary, whose dreams and idylls have no lasting therapeutic value and are in fact part of the problem.)

Some thirty years earlier, Sartre had already pushed similar techniques even further to get at much deeper issues. *La Nausée* (Nausea) 1938, recounts Roquentin's contempt for the bourgeoisie of Bouville, i.e., "Mudtown," who give themselves over to the rituals of social etiquette on Sunday walks after mass. The scenes of salutation are in the comic tradition of seventeenth-century social observation, and the resemblance to La Bruyère is greatly enhanced by metaphors of masks and of crabs, and particularly by the presence of the *Autodidacte* or Self-Taught Man. A creature straight out of the *Characters* (e.g., XIII, 2) by way of Flaubert's *Bouvard and Pécuchet* (1881), he bears an allegorical title rather than a name, and, instead of living spontaneously and in the moment, he devotes himself to reading the Encyclopedia from A to Z! Moreover, the book is Roquentin's diary, a form he has chosen in preference to the historical biography on which he had been working until recently, and the novel is a disavowal by Sartre of various other narrative forms. But despite La Bruyère's self-conscious relationship to other writers and his adaptation of certain traditional genres, the author of the *Characters* does not make so radical and philosophical a distinction between one form and another, and his nostalgia for an earlier density and personal integrity is a type of bad faith compared to the lucid recognition of man's nothingness which was a basic tenet of Sartrian Existentialism.

In our day, the various elements of the *caractère* tradition come closest together in what could be broadly called social psychology, particularly a number of works where the coordinates of self and society are in a relation of tension and interdetermination, and where that relationship is perceived on the level of a code.

David Riesman's notion of inner- and other-directed (*The Lonely Crowd*, 1950) applies extremely well to the world of the *Characters*, and one even wonders whether La Bruyère's definition of virtue is not basically a case of tradition-direction. Krailsheimer's introduction alludes pertinently to Stephen Potter's *Gamesmanship* (1948). One could also find parallels to seventeenth-century tragic situations in R. D. Laing's *Knots* (1970), and La Rochefoucauld was analyzing the same socio-psychological illusions which Eric Berne portrayed in *Games People Play* (1964), a title applicable in general to the range of human behavior as seen by the *moralistes*. And is La Bruyère's great lord become a petty prince (XIV, 7) so very different from the highest level of incompetence which Peter and Hull studied tongue-in-cheek in *The Peter Principle* (1969)? [11]

What has changed since La Bruyère becomes clearer if we compare "the features and countenance of a man who, alone among mortal men, possesses such a plum!" (XIII, 1) with the prune described by Vance Packard in *The Hidden Persuaders*.[12] Motivational research in the 1950's showed that prunes were not selling because their image was one of age and desiccation. The subsequent advertising campaigns emphasized color, gaiety and youth, and the consumer's conception of the prune changed as a function of its surroundings. The elements are similar (person, object, and code), but the relationship is perceived at a different stage and the dynamic process of extension studied on its way back, so to speak. The man whose passion for rare and unusual things led him to restrict his whole outlook to a particular species of fruit, is only implicitly present in Packard's analysis, which deals more with the system of images on the basis of which the prune's social presence succeeds or fails. Moreover, in its furthest modern development (structuralism), the code becomes autonomous: if not completely divorced from those who created it, at the very least a stable system already in place, and a more determinant force than any specific and individual human weakness.

In retrospect, it is no accident that Roland Barthes should have chosen to preface an edition of the *Characters*, since his own work has been one long inquiry into the function and social significance of signs. He is the author of a *System of Fashion,* but even more reminiscent of fashion in La Bruyère's sense of social usage is his *Mythologies*.[18] Defined as signs whose second-level content is ideological and resolutely condemned as a bourgeois phenomenon, the mythologies in his analysis—as in La Bruyère's—often seem to be illustrations of a foregone socio-political conclusion, but it is nonetheless a subtle and erudite study of the ways man is defined and revealed in his relationship to various public and seemingly innocuous manifestations of political, social, and cultural trends. Compared to the *Characters*, the work is modern in its abstruse terminology but more convincingly in its postulation of a system rather than a collection of objects which man may or may not successfully command.

In *The Uses of Literacy* (London: Chatto & Windus, 1957), Richard Hoggart draws a composite but detailed portrait of the English working class: its furnishings, speech, amusements, etc. His argument is more subtle than La Bruyère's and applies to a social group which was virtually anonymous in the earlier literature, but Hoggart uses similar portrait techniques and shows a very similar concern for values perverted or lost. Asserting that improved living conditions have been accompanied by cultural changes which are often a deterioration, he shows in particular how commercial journalism has ceased to be simply an extension of a class or the result of its taste, and has become at least as much its manipulator, preying cynically on the qualities of the "common man" troubled by a world in flux.

James Agee and Walker Evans' *Let Us Now Praise Famous Men* (New York: Houghton Mifflin, 1941) began as a report on daily life in the heart of the cotton belt, and became a poetic and moving search for an adequate portrayal of the sharecropper in the details of his features, clothes, dwellings, and speech. Agee's wish that the text be read aloud recalls oratorical technique in La Bruyère, and other similarities include his polemical remarks on tradition ("Intermission"), his apostrophizing, and his irony, although he defends his subjects to somewhat the same degree that La Bruyère criticized his. The work is modern in the sense that the scandal of peasant life is no longer contained in a passing remark (XI, 128), but is a whole world to be explored from within. The author's explicit reflections on the inadequacy of typology and the impossibility of "representing" a human phenomenon of such proportions are further indications of a less class-restricted but no less morally urgent turn of mind. (See, for example, his assertion in the preface that author and reader are of the same "human actuality" which is his subject. Compare also his adaptation of the biblical "Famous Men" to La Bruyère's models or even to the rather stuffy idealizations of Steinbeck's *Grapes of Wrath.*) Finally, his use of the present tense is far more unusual in Eng-- lish than was La Bruyère's in French, and his statement that the photographs in the volume are to be considered a mode equivalent to words rather than their illustration places him squarely in the semiological tradition.

Barthes' most recent effort along these lines is *The Realm of Signs* (*L'Empire des signes*), Geneva: Skira, 1970. "Without the slightest pretentions at representing or analyzing reality (those are the preoccupations of Western discourse), I can nevertheless single out somewhere in the world a certain number of features (a graphic and linguistic term) and from those features deliberately form a system. I shall call that system: Japan" (preface). It often seems that what was once mere hyperbole in La Bruyère has become a high-flown jargon with Barthes. Nonetheless, striking similarities include a viewpoint which is ethically removed from the system to be described, but aesthetically dependent on it, and the idea of a semiotic system as a foreign country (and vice versa). And like Agee, Barthes puts linguistic and graphic features on an equal footing: the seventeenth-century analogy between painting and literary portraits has been subsumed into the general category of signs.

IV   *Complementarity*

In the preface to his edition of the *Characters* (29), Claude Roy compares the portrait of Ménalque (XI, 7) to a series of sketches of sight gags provoking laughter in the same way as Charlie Chaplin or Buster Keaton. The parallel is suggestive but more relevant to a few

specific remarks than to the general outlook of La
Bruyère's work. It is the repetitive nature of Chaplin's
and Keaton's comedy that most likens them to *caractère*
and even more to farce, which Roy mentions. A movie
maker would be equally well advised to adopt a stop-
action technique to suggest a link with portraiture and
to get at the perpetual posturing of La Bruyère's subjects. (Cf. Saint-Simon, who uses brutal closeups, but
also makes extraordinary use of the "pan" shot, sweeping
across a whole gallery of faces and attitudes. The most
cinematographic aspect of La Bruyère's technique is in
fact the range and scope he achieves through *montage*
of a number of different and separate moments of a
character's activity.) Moreover, since La Bruyère's contemporaries seem to have read his work with "real" people in mind, it would be more appropriate to cite W. C.
Fields, whom his viewers always rather suspected of
playing himself, or a "key" novel dealing with celebrities
of the day.

The social typologies of Balzac's time had their "illus-
trators" in Daumier and Gavarni, but even when they
dealt with the professions their representation relied
much more on physical caricature, which is in fact quite
rare in the *Characters*. (In his way, Ingres' Monsieur
Bertin is a better example of full social presence.) Not
surprisingly, we must go back almost to La Bruyère's
time to find the closest pictorial equivalent. More than
any other work, the characters, techniques and vision of
Hogarth, particularly in *Marriage à la Mode* (1745),
recall the *Characters*.[14] The artist's vision admittedly
extends deeper into the lower reaches of society than
does La Bruyère's, and his realism imparts a far more
literal morbidity to his work, but the resemblances are
nonetheless striking and numerous. Individual subjects

are perceived in terms of type and class, although "keys" were also published. The characters are defined by their physiognomies, gestures and surroundings, and each plate freezes the action in a quasi-theatrical attitude. Moreover, the plates are so fraught with significant detail that critics often speak of "reading" Hogarth, rather like the reverse temptation to put La Bruyère's characters on a stage. Finally, there is the same concern with moral decadence, although the result obviously belongs to descriptive or illustrative ethics, and we cannot always be sure the artist's ethical concerns were not eclipsed by aesthetic considerations. Such in any case is how his work is seen today, and is my own viewpoint on La Bruyère.

CHAPTER 9

Conclusion

WHAT makes the *Characters* of interest is La
Bruyère's ability to perceive and explicitly to
project a vision of the relationship between man and
his social and concrete surroundings, and to have seen
that relationship as not only causal but symbiotic, a
process rather than simply the elements with which one
satirized a certain social type or literary genre. He
attributed it primarily to an inner emptiness, the loss
of an earlier self which he saw in moral terms whereas
modern analysts focus more closely on the system itself,
but the difference is a shift of emphasis rather than
qualitative.

Erving Goffman's *The Presentation of Self in Everyday
Life*, for example, is a more strictly functional approach
to social conduct and his delineation of moral is somewhat flatter than La Bruyère's, referring essentially to
a notion of social "rightness" rather than the consistency
with a presocial self which seems to be La Bruyère's
ideal.[1] His study of how such values come to be con-
ferred and maintained, however, is so detailed, sensitive,
and consistent with French writing of the late seventeenth century as to seem the social-psychological formulation of the literary concerns of that period. He refers
frequently to the testimony of books on etiquette, the
experience of domestics, and anecdotes from Sir Fred-

erick Ponsonby's *Recollections of Three Reigns* (New York: Dutton, 1952), as examples that show life as "a dramatically enacted thing" (72). Page after page analyzes not only role-playing but "the crucial discrepancy between our all-too-human selves and our socialized selves" (56).

Readers familiar with the French literary tradition should also consult Goffman's observations on high-level conflicts (55) and the contingencies of being an exalted person (120), and they may also see possible applications of his remarks on the physical confines of social life (Racine, Saint-Simon), competence vs. dependence (Racine), and the ramifications of discreditable activity (Molière).[2] Even closer to La Bruyère, and in addition to the basic metaphor of theater, are his analyses of life as an "information game" (8) and the techniques and difficulties of "impression management" (108–237). He wisely observes, however, that not every culture leads an indoor social life (244), and adds a caution regarding "any attempt to characterize our own society as a whole with respect to dramaturgical practices" (245).

The latter remark underscores the major difference between the two works: The modern recognizes subgroups within the society he is analyzing as did La Bruyère, but declines to extrapolate that society beyond its time and space in order to see it as the repository of "mankind." (That reticence, which is also in a sense a call to specialization, is basically an acquisition of the eighteenth century.) It is also true that the position of the observer has changed. When Goffman says "we have distinguished three crucial roles on the basis of function: those who perform; those performed; and outsiders who neither perform in the show nor observe it" (144), he is describing a social situation familiar to readers of La Bruyère, but without the full rhetorical context of the *Characters*. In other words, who and where is "we"?

The two works, finally, are complementary. Goffman's approach sharpens and structures the awareness of a reader inclined to relegate the insights and techniques of an earlier age to mere literary history. The same is true of a receptive reading of La Bruyère for those who find relevance only in the latest developments of social science. Whether or not there is anything new under the sun depends on convention and mode, or as La Bruyère put it, "It has all been said . . . but I have made it mine."

Notes and References

Chapter One

1. On the historical setting, see Hugh Kearney, "Social Structure and Social Change," in *The Seventeenth Century*, ed. John Cruickshank, vol. 2 of *French Literature and Its Background* (London: Oxford University Press, 1969), 66–81; Paul Hazard, *The European Mind, the Critical Years, 1680–1715* (New Haven: Yale University Press, 1953), trans. of *La Crise de conscience européenne* (Paris: Boivin, 1935); W. H. Lewis, *The Splendid Century* (Garden City: Doubleday Anchor, 1953); John Lough, *An Introduction to Seventeenth Century France* (London: Longmans, 1954).

2. *Essais Critiques*, p. 226. On French neoclassicism and the literary public, see Antoine Adam, *Grandeur and Illusion. French Literature and Society 1600–1715* (London: Weidenfield and Nicolson, 1972); Erich Auerbach,, "La Cour et la ville," in trans. Ralph Manheim, *Scenes from the Drama of European Literature* (New York: Meridian, 1959), pp. 133–79; Peter Brooks, *The Novel of Worldliness* (Princeton: Princeton University Press, 1969), pp. 44–93; Cruickshank, *op. cit.*, 82–98; Lough, *op. cit.*, pp. 173–267; W. G. Moore, *French Classical Literature* (London: Oxford University Press, 1961); Suzanne Rossat-Mignod. "Situation matérielle et sociale des écrivains" in eds. Annie Ubersfeld et Roland Desné, *Manuel d'histoire littéraire de la France, tome II: 1600–1715* (Paris: Editions sociales, 1966), 52–70.

3. On the *moralistes*, see Paul Bénichou, *Morales du Grand Siècle* (Paris: Gallimard, 1948) trans. Elizabeth Hughes, *Man and Ethics* (Garden City: Doubleday Anchor, 1971); H. Chamard, "Three French Moralists of the Seventeenth

Century: La Rochefoucauld, Pascal, La Bruyère," *Rice Institute Pamphlets* 18 (1931), 1–13; Hugo Friederich, *Montaigne* (Paris: Gallimard, 1968), pp. 189–95; Krailsheimer and Van Delft.

4. The best-known English character-writers at the time seem to have been Joseph Hall, *Characters of Vice and Virtue* (1610, trans. 1612), and John Earle, *Micro-cosmographie* 1628, trans. 1654). See Benjamin Boyce, *The Theophrastan Character in England to 1642* (Cambridge: Harvard University Press, 1947) and *The Polemic Character 1640–61* (Lincoln: University of Nebraska Press, 1955). An authoritative bibliography is by Chester N. Greenough, *A Bibliography of the Theophrastan Character in English* (Cambridge: Harvard University Press, 1947), and there is an anthology of the character tradition: Richard Aldington, *A Book of Characters* (London: G. Routledge & Sons, 1924).

For Theophrastus, see Warren Anderson, trans., *Theophrastus: The Character Sketches* (Kent, Ohio: Kent State University Press, 1970), or R. G. Ussher, ed., *The Characters of Theophrastus* (London: Macmillan, 1960), both with informative introductions.

Chapter Three

1. References to Pascal indicate both the Brunschvicg and Lafuma numberings.

2. Equally suggestive is a Cartesian development from simple to complex, which Laubriet proposed (512) and which Van Delft apparently sees as the table of organization [*organigramme*] missing in the discussion of human nature (62–63). Unfortunately, he seems to jump from analysis of a few rather atypical remarks to a view of the whole, which in turn he bases on a simple equivalence between chapter headings and subjects. The necessity of the schema with respect to the work's structure remains to be shown. Is "On the Heart" less complex than "On Judgment," or "On Preaching" more so than "On Society and Conversation" or "On Mankind"?

3. See Appendix I. For interpretation of the changes, see

Notes and References

Jasinski; Lange, 392–96; Laubriet, 502–4; Koppisch; Kuentz, 12–15; Van Delft, 15–51.

4. See Goyet, 4–6; Van Delft, 55–56.

5. Other general remarks include: I, 1; II, 1, 37, 41; III, 1, 5, 11, 53, 54; IV, 1, 7, 72, 73; V, 1; VII, 1, 4; VIII, 2, 12, 19, 52, 101; IX, 1, 47; X, 1, 8, 33; XI, 1, 4, 15, 18, 64, 69, 75, 76, 87, 99, 113, 131, 147, 156; XII, 12, 22, 27, 71; XIII, 1, 5 ;XIV, 8, 18; XV, 1, 30; XVI, 1, 9, 49.

With respect to a discussion of the book's organization, I am referring here to remarks which are not only general, but which have an explicative value as well. They may lead into the discussion, or in some cases be a conclusion, but they must act in some way as a principle of organization, a key as well as a summary ("On the Heart" is full of maxims and truths, but those in "On Mankind" have much greater range and resonance.) They are centers or epicenters, sources rather than headings.

The models of wisdom or conduct which La Bruyère proposes are situated in an ideal and hypothetical realm outside or beyond the particular/general continuum and I have therefore discussed them under *vision*.

6. There are other examples of *modulation* between chapters. Conversation is one medium of exchange, money is another (V–VI); the pulpit is a link between custom and theology (XIV–XV–XVI). One could even contend that the chapter on the highest of mortals can only be followed by a discussion of men in general (X–XI).

7. See, for example, the magistracy (*robe* in the original): I, 3; II, 29; III, 29; VI, 5; VII, 5–9, 10; IX, 40; XIV, 41–55; XV, 26, 27. As "fixed" a figure as the sovereign (X) appears elsewhere (II, 33; VIII, 57; IX, 24, 27, 29, 39, 42, 43; XI, 35; XII, 87, 107, 118, 119; XIII, 27, 62; XVI, 3, 28), as does a less theoretical one like Corneille (I, 30, 54; II, 24; XII, 14, 17, 56).

8. On money and riches, see also IV, 20, 59–62; VIII, 21, 34, 55, 62, 84 ,98; XI, 29; XII, 14, 17, 21; XIV, 1–3, 10; in connection with ambition: VI, 3, 49, 50, 59, 62. Ambition elsewhere: II, 43; III, 59; IV, 74–76; VIII, 43, 70, 72; XI, 24, 27; XII, 69, 114, 115.

9. In a slightly different perspective, Van Delft distin-

guishes between permanent themes, maintained throughout the editions: social criticism, the art of writing, defense of religion, observation of ridiculous behavior, denunciation of vanity. And a series of newer topics which represent a broadening of the writer's curiosity: current political affairs, questions of language, nature, family relations, *précieux* controversies, childhood, etc. (49). He also discerns leit motifs which give a "second element of unity" to the work: disdain for appearances; independent judgment; and condemnation of his contemporaries' most cherished values (51).

10. See also Jean Starobinski, "La Rochefoucauld et les morales substitutives," *Nouvelle Revue Française*, 163–64 (1966), 212.

Chapter Four

1. Comparisons of emotions and/or personal qualities: II, 42; III, 48; IV, 4, 10; VI, 38; XI, 78; XII, 1, 5, 8, 56, 69. Individuals: I, 38–41, 45, 54; XII, 11, 14–17, 19, 22, 105; XIII, 10. The various definitions and contrastive evaluations of types (social, economic, aesthetic) are far more prominent and very typical of an outlook, prevalent in La Bruyère's time, which constantly sought greater precision and refinement through the juxtaposition of fixed and known quantities. I, 35–37, 43, 61; II, 4, 30, 31; III *passim.*; V, 2, 69; VI, 12, 49, 83; VII, 16; IX, 12, 18, 23–25; 28, 29, 47, 53; XI, 53, 66, 96; XII *passim.*; XIII, 2, 26; XIV, 4; XV, 26.

2. I, 20, 59; II, 9, 20; III, 17, 18, 30, 59, 71, 78–80; IV, 4, 6, 7, 11, 19, 23, 24, 30–40, 63, 71, 74; V, 1, 48, 57; VI, 45; VIII, 33–37; XI, 13, 64, 108–11, 150, 153; XII, 1, 57; XIII, 21; XIV, 52.

3. Ellipses: IV, 34; VIII, 55; XII, 56, 87. Observations: II, 2; IV, 37; XI, 19, 33, 36, 42, 48, 64, 76, 99, 154; XII, 10, 56, 98; XVI, 15, 34, 35, 43, 44. La Bruyère explicitly contradicts Pascal in XII, 105.

4. I, 51, 52; X, 7, 12, 24; XIV, 17–73; XV, 26; XVI, 44–47. The firstperson references in the *Characters* are discussed in Chapter V.

5. La Bruyère's "sermons" include: II, 11; III, 42, 43; V, 50; VI, 58, 74, 78; VII, 20; IX, 25; X, 9, 21; XI, 49, 119;

Notes and References

XIII, 23; XIV, 19; See also Chapter V on the rhetorical situation.

6. *Ad Herennium*, trans. Harry Caplan (Loeb Classical Library, Cambridge: Harvard University Press, 1954), IV, 49–50. On portrait and *caractère*, see Brooks, *Novel of Worldliness, passim.*; Cruickshank, "Aphorism and Portraiture" in *The Seventeenth Century*, pp. 136–51; Jean D. Lafond, "Les Techniques du portrait dans le 'Recueil des portraits et éloges' de 1659," *Cahiers de l'Association Internationale des Études Françaises* 18 (1966), 139–48 and discussion, 270–75.

7. In the original, the word *caractère* appears in I, 24, 52; II, 36; V, 1, 13, 20, 28, 37; VI, 69; VII, 7; VIII, 96; IX, 26; X, 12, 13; XI, 7, 52, 140, 141, 147; XII, 26; XV, 24; XVI, 36.

8. Name-dropping: V, 8, 73, 75, 82; VI, 21; VII, 10, 12; VIII, 15, 20, 57, 59; IX, 23; X, 11; XII, 56, 99; XIV, 9, 16; cf. X, 21, 27, 35. Self-inflation: II, 10; V, 14; VI, 12, 51; VII, 10; VIII, 20; IX, 50; XI, 67; XIV, 26. On jargon: I, 21, 29; V, 6, 7, 69; VII, 4, 10; XIII, 2; XIV, 3, 50. Incompetence: II, 38; V, 21; VIII, 61; XI, 83; cf. XII, 56.

9. See other italics (VI, 56; X, 11; XI, 7; XIV, 99) and several other expressions: "only they know how to judge, etc." (I, 24); "avenge" (III, 62); "dear husband"(III, 73); "There are some things . . ." (V, 8); "deign" (V, 13); "all about . . . horrible chaos . . . through and through . . ." (V, 74); "man of means" (VI, 15); "Why did his father not die" (VI, 21); "so useful to the State" (VIII, 19); "horrible" (XI, 122); "A man in disgrace can do nothing right" (XII, 93); " 'Tis beyond all bearing." (XII, 99); "fine . . . dreadful" (XII, 115). Like all ironic devices this one is difficult to circumscribe, particularly since La Bruyère makes copious use of indirect statement (e.g., III, 81; V, 8, 74, 82; VI, 7, 26; VIII, 20; IX, 15; X, 11; XIII, 2; XV, 23), and because a single subordinate conjunction may introduce a series of statements. How to interpret parts of II, 39; III, 62; V, 13; VI, 56; VII, 5; XII, 25; XIV, 36, 37?

For an historical and stylistic discussion, see Dorrit Cohn, "Narrated Monologue," *Comparative Literature* XIII (Spring 1966), 97–112; and Stephen Ullmann, "Reported Speech in Flaubert," *Style in the French Novel* (Cambridge: Cam-

bridge University Press, 1957), pp. 94–120. The latter sees
La Fontaine alone among neoclassical practitioners of the
device.
10. Physical details: II, 26, 28; III, 6; VI, 17, 78, 79;
IX, 3; XI, 94; XIII, 2, 14, 16. Actions: II, 37, 43; III, 73, 79;
IV, 52; V, 10, 12, 24; VI, 50, 56, 60, 68; VII, 4, 18, 22, 42;
IX, 15, 50; X, 11; XI, 7, 120, 142; XIII, 2, 21, 22, 24. See
also: III, 45, 74; V, 5, 14, 27, 50, 65, 74; VI, 13, 38, 58, 69,
72, 75; VII, 18, 21, 26; IX, 13, 20; X, 3, 20; XI, 1, 4, 9, 18,
24, 27, 50, 76, 113, 114, 127, 131; XII, 9, 56, 77, 119; XIII, 10;
XIV, 13, 34, 35, 64, 73; XVI, 21, 26, 33.
11. "Typical time": II, 37–39; V, 8, 9, 13, 24; VI, 12, 16;
VII, 12; VIII, 15; IX, 48, 50; XII, 64; XIV, 64. Cf. examples
of progression from beginning to end, a temporal sequence
usually expressing a "career" (*chemin*) which La Bruyère
sees as invasion and usurpation: VI, 7, 15, 16, 19, 21, 27,
35, 60, 69; VIII, 57, 68, 95; XI, 156; XII, 59; XIII, 25.
12. On hypothetical extension and potential, se also: I, 29,
52, 63; III, 6; V, 5, 11–14, 24, 74, 75; VI, 7, 9, 11, 25, 29, 35,
37, 38, 45, 56, 78 ,83; VII, 4, 10, 13–15; VIII, 12, 26, 50, 58,
61, 79; IX, 2, 15, 41, 48; X, 11, 21, 24; XI, 7, 121, 122; XII,
56, 60, 99, 119; XIII, 2, 11, 21, 24; XIV, 16, 53, 64, 71.
13. For explanations at the beginning, see: I, 37, 52; III,
43, 45; V, 11, 27; VIII, 20, 22, 46; IX, 34; X, 12; XI, 67, 89,
115, 142; XV, 29. In the middle: II, 39, 40; V, 7; VII, 13;
VIII, 19; XII, 22; XIII, 24. Beginning and end: II, 13; V, 12;
VIII, 28, 99; XI, 121; XII, 21; XIII, 2. Presentation without
explanation: I, 29; II, 38; V, 6, 13, 74; VI, 21; VII, 10; IX,
20, 48; X, 11; XI, 96; XII, 64; XIII, 9; XIV, 68, 73.
14. Interpretation: I, 23–25; II, 28, 35, 38; III, 29, 36;
V, 7, 8; VI, 20, 29, 43, 83; VII, 7; VIII, 46, 48, 66, 67; IX, 2,
9, 50; X, 12, 20; XI, 50, 83, 104, 108, 114, 122; XII, 21, 64,
115; XIII, 2, 16; XIV, 25, 26, 28, 33, 54; XV, 18, 23; XVI, 22.
Time out of control: I, 21; V, 9, 82; VI, 62, 78; XI, 25, 105.
Death: III, 7, 45; IV, 66; VI, 17, 39, 79; VII, 12; VIII, 22;
XI, 121, 124; XII, 78; cf. II, 1; IIIfi 79.
15. Hyperbole: II, 17, 32, 40; III, 76; V, 3, 12, 46, 74, 75;
VI, 12, 21, 28, 35, 47, 58, 80, 83; VII, 14, 18, 22, 57, 59;
VIII, 62; IX, 15, 32, 48; X, 11; XI, 7, 121, 122, 125, 143;
XII, 12, 56; XIV, 25, 26, 64. Images of machinery: III, 49;

Notes and References

VI, 25, VIII, 19, 32, 43, 64, 65; XI, 142; XII, 17, 56, 73; XIV, 28; cf. XV, 26. Commerce: I, 62; III, 48; V, 75; VI, 28, 43; VIII, 12, 16, 62, 81, 83; IX, 50; XI, 12, 131; XVI, 4; cf. V, 37; X, 10. Animals, insects, etc.: II, 38, 40; III, 5, 49; V, 3; VI, 12; VII, 4, 15; VIII, 12, 19, 46; X, 12, 20; XI, 128, 142; XII, 11, 22, 119; XIV, 25; XVI, 38. Sickness: II, 43; III, 16; V, 71; VIII, 14, 101; IX, 15; X, 7; XI, 148, 151, 158; XII, 41; XIII, 2. Tyranny and enslavement: I, 60; II, 11; III, 45; VIII, 62, 67, 69, 70; XII, 119; XIII, 1, 3; XIV, 64; XVI, 9. La Bruyère discusses metaphor and hyperbole in I, 55. As Doubrovsky, Kirsch and Brody have pointed out, the Cartesian definition of animals as mere machines, and his distinction between extensive matter and cognitive matter, almost certainly formed the intellectual backdrop of La Bruyère's use of metaphor and metonymy.

Chapter Five

1. Kirsch's excellent remarks on signs and the "reified society" (pp. 77–101) cover much the same ground as *code*, but my discussion differs with respect to a few details and more generally in its integration into a rhetorical vision of things which seems to me essential to the full meaning of the *Characters*.

2. For similar attention to language and names, see: II, 28; III, 36; V, 63, 65, 66, 82; VI, 36; VII, 7, 21; IX, 8, 23, 37; X, 10, 27; XII, 11; XIII, 2; XIV, 19, 50, 58, 73; XVI, 21.

3. Theater, mask, and makeup: II, 11; III, 33; V, 30, 75; VI, 25, 31; VII, 3, 11, 19; VIII, 17, 32, 43, 48, 61, 99; IX, 40, 50; X, 20; XI, 131, 140; XII, 27–29, 104, 115; XIII, 6, 12, 28; XV, 1. On the history of classical metaphor, see Ernst Robert Curtius, *European Literature and the Latin Middle Ages*, trans. Willard R. Trask, Bollingen Series (New York: Pantheon, 1953).

4. On "blindness" and discernment, etc.: II, 5, 27, 37; II, 5, 7; V, 14, 31, 81; VI, 21, 53; VIII, 13, 39, 44, 51, 83, 94, 100; IX, 13, 20; X, 12, 35; XI, 12, 25, 83, 94, 156; XII, 20, 27, 36, 57; XV, 27. La Bruyère focuses more on the manifestations and results of "blindness" than did La Rochefoucauld, but a number of remarks refer to a self-deception not un-

like that in the *Maximes*: I, 49; II, 40; III, 7, 44; V, 11, 82, 84; VII, 10, 11; VIII, 82; X, 11; XII, 72; XIV, 4. Cf. reciprocal dupery as the opposite of social harmony (V, 58).

5. See Henri Coulet, "La Rochefoucauld ou la peur d'être dupe" in *Hommage au Doyen Etienne Gros,* Publications de la Faculté des Lettres d'Aix-en-Provence (Gap: Imprimerie Louis-Jean, 1959), pp. 105–12; Friederich, *Montaigne,* pp. 223–27; Jeanson; Jean-Yves Pouilloux, *lire les "essais" de Montaigne* (Paris: Maspéro, 1969), pp. 112–18.

6. Corrections, etc.: I, 34; IV, 73; VI, 34; VIII, 10, 19, 32, 54, 80, 83, 84; IX, 29, 34, 45; X, 21; XI, 23, 139, 142, 143; XII, 56, 77, 80, 93, 94; XIII, 2, 14; XIV, 19, 36, 50, 56, 70. See Chapter 4, n. 10, on accumulation and juxtaposition. The other oratorical devices are too numerous to be listed here: Taken together, exclamation and apposition occur over one hundred times, and there are more than 150 instances of rhetorical questions and apostrophe.

7. On the undiscerning public, see: II, 27; V, 12; VI, 10; VIII, 16, 20; XI, 26, 71; XII, 59, 79, 98; XIII, 24, 28; XV, 5, 27; XVI, 9, 26. Cf. XII, 61; XV, 10.

8. See Marmier on antithesis and compensation (pp. 235–6) and Kirsch on the "law of contraries" (pp. 16–30). Worthy models defined in the negative are: II, 11, 13; V, 20, 23, 50; VII, 15; VIII, 31, 66, 83; XII, 2, 29, 73. Cf. III, 36, where a negative phenomenon is described via the positive.

9. On *peuple*, see Krailsheimer (p. 207) and Koppisch (pp. 71–77). See also I, 8, 30, 32, 46; V, 71; VI, 28, 30–32; IX, 1, 18, 22, 23, 41; X, 5, 6, 8, 10, 23, 24, 27, 29, 31, 32, 35; XI, 97; XII, 5, 22, 88, 115, 117; XIII, 3, 8; XIV, 4, 54; XV, 10, 13; XVI, 5, 22.

10. Shift to a moral plane: II, 10, 20, 27, 43; III, 38, 46; IV, 52; V, 31; VI, 18, 26, 68; VIII, 53; IX, 3, 25, 51; X, 29; XI, 147; XII, 38; XIII, 22; XVI, 29. See also Chapter 4, n. 14.

11. As Kaminker (p. 25) and Stewart (p. 248) point out, *honnête homme* retains in some cases its earlier meaning of general personal excellence (V, 20; VIII, 9). Other references indicate an excellence seen from the outside, as a category to which one belongs (I, 24; II, 25; III, 13; V, 68; XI, 14; XII, 30), resulting in a formalism detached from

personal worth which is one of the obstacles to "integrity" (XII, 55; XIV, 37).

12. Van Delft (p. 133) very pertinently quotes the following passage from Chamfort, a *moraliste* of the eighteenth century: "The man of the world, the friend of fortune and even the lover of glory, all draw before them a straight line leading to an unknown point. The wise man, his own best friend, describes a circular line running back to himself." *Maximes et Pensées, Caractères et Anecdotes*, ed. P. Grosclaude (Paris: Imprimerie Nationale, 1953), I, 163. The ideal of self-sufficiency and moderation goes back at least to Aristotle's *Ethics*. See Herschel Baker, *The Image of Man* (New York: Harper & Row, 1947 2nd ed. 1961), pp. 61–68.

13. I, 53; II, 11, 18–20, 22, 32, 43, 44; III, 2, 48, 72, 85; V, 31, 43; VI, 16, 56–58; VII, 15; VIII, 1, 22, 53, 56, 85, 96; IX, 12 ,13, 41, 46, 50, 53; X, 9, 35; XI, 2, 3, 14, 28, 65, 69, 84, 93, 103, 128, 147, 148; XII, 8, 27–30, 74, 93, 112; XIII, 5, 21, 23, 28, 31; XIV, 15, 31; XV, 13; XVI, 35, 47. Virolle rightly sees the ethic of the *Characters* as Christian humanism. On the other hand, he is more concerned with synonyms of *vertu* than with the distribution of the word, which appears at least as often in the plural, i.e., in the sense of "qualities." That is why I prefer to define it functionally rather than nominatively, and place it like "merit" under *integrity*.

14. "La Bruyère was always disturbed . . . by the question of the real relationship between permanence and change. *Deux choses toutes contraires nous préviennent également, l'habitude et la nouveauté* ["Two completely opposite things predispose and deceive us, habit and novelty," (XII, 4)]. He believed that there were standards. He knew that his Christianity gave him an anchor. But he did not know where to fix the line from his anchor . . ." E. B. O. Borgerhoff, *The Freedom of French Classicism* (Princeton: Princeton University Press, 1950), p. 215.

15. As the opposite of congruence, moderation and propriety, disproportion is the general category to which hyperbole and metaphor belong and of which the collectors (XIII, 2) are the most notable example. See also: II, 27, 40; III, 7, 76; V, 12, 47; VI, 5, 40, 49, 58, 59, 71; VII, 7, 8, 10, 16;

VIII *passim.*, e.g., 62, 66, 97; IX, 8, 19, 28, 48; X, 18; XI, 31, 85, 130, 140, 141; XII, 41, 56; XIII, 1–3, 6, 14, 15; XIV, 1, 23, 24, 26, 30, 31, 35, 51, 63, 64; XV, 22, 23; XVI, 3, 6, 16, 22, 24, 25.

There are also several references to a resemblance and/or confusion between men and women: I, 52; II, 3; III, 52, 76; VII, 20; VIII, 17, 61; IX, 48; XI, 7, 155; XIII, 14; XIV, 16; cf. III, 13. La Bruyère uses *aliénation* and *manie* (VIII, 50, 61) to mean becoming other than what one is, but more as eccentricity and folly than in their modern sense. This in no way diminishes, however, the pernicious importance of the Other, as Koppisch has demonstrated.

Chapter Eight

1. For surveys that are similar but which diverge from my own and from each other at numerous points, see Donald Furber, *La Bruyère in France 1696–1751* (New Haven: Diss. Yale University, 1955), and Richard, pp. 184–215. Brooks, *The Novel of Worldliness*, traces the history of the portrait in the novel.

2. The numbers in parentheses refer to the volume and pages of the authoritative French edition of the *Mémoires*, ed. Gonzague Truc (Paris: Bibliothèque de la Pléiade, Gallimard, 1947–61), 7 vols.

3. See Michel Guggenheim, "Sous le regard perçant de Saint-Simon," *Modern Language Notes* 82 (1967), 291–305.

4. See Erich Auerbach, *Mimesis*, trans. Ralph Manheim (Garden City: Doubleday Anchor, 1953), pp. 365–82.

5. Compare also *Spectator* 69 on the stock exchange with Voltaire's *Philosophical Letters* (e.g., No. 10), published in 1734 and the first literary attempt in France at enfranchising the bourgeois proudly and with a clear conscience. Even then the writer was obliged to do so via a portrait of English society which he hoped would rub off on his countrymen, and the book was still condemned.

6. See Margaret Turner, "The Influence of La Bruyère on the 'Tatler' and the 'Spectator,'" *Modern Language Review* 48 (1953), 10–16; and Richmond P. Bond, *The Tatler. The*

Notes and References

Making of a Literary Journal (Cambridge: Harvard University Press, 1971), pp. 143–50.

7. On both the general and particular aspects of these problems, see Brooks, *op. cit.*, pp. 94–141; and Jean Rousset, "Marivaux ou la structure du double registre," *Forme et signification* (Paris: J. Corti, 1962), pp. 45–64.

8. On the scientistic intent of Balzac's foreward, see Auerbach, *Mimesis*, pp. 413–25; and Peter Demetz, "Balzac and the Zoologists: A Concept of the Type" in *The Disciplines of Criticism* (New Haven: Yale University Press, 1968), pp. 397–418.

9. *Balzac romancier* (Paris. Plon, 1950), pp. 134–140.

10. In practice, social signs and symptoms are not so far removed. Editors sometimes group under *The Pathology of Social Life*, "On Fashionable Expressions," "Treatise on Elegant Living," "Theory of Walking," and "Treatise on Modern Stimulants." All are written in a combination of aphorisms, examples and longer observations, and closely resemble the *Characters* in form and theme. As such, they are what we would call semiology (linguistic usage, dress and personal style, body language) rather than pathology.

11. Riesman, *The Lonely Crowd* (New Haven: Yale University Press, 1950); Stephen Potter, *Gamesmanship* (New York: Holt, Rinehart & Winston, 1948); Eric Berne, *Games people Play* (New York: Grove Press, 1964); Laurence J. Peter and Raymond Hull, *The Peter Principle* (New York: William Morrow & Company, 1969).

12. Vance Packard, *The Hidden Persuaders* (New York: McKay, 1957), pp. 137–40.

13. *Système de la mode* (Paris: Seuil, 1967); *Mythologies* (Paris: Seuil, 1957), transl. Annette Lavers, *Mythologies*, New York: Hill and Wang, 1972.

14. See Arthur Wensinger, trans. and ed. with W. B. Coley, *Hogarth on High Life: The "Marriage à la Mode" Series from Georg Christoph Lichtenberg's "Commentaries"* (Middletown: Wesleyan University Press, 1970).

Chapter Nine

1. "Whatever it is that generates the human want for social contact and for companionship, the effect seems to take two forms. . . ." Goffman, *The Presentation of Self in Everyday Life* (Garden City: Doubleday Anchor, 1959), p. 206. Professor Goffman distinguishes between character, self and performer, pp. 252–55.

2. Goffman, pp. xi, 194, and 64 respectively.

Selected Bibliography

PRIMARY SOURCES

1. Books by La Bruyère

Oeuvres. Ed. G. Servois. Paris: Hachette, 1865–78. The definitive historical edition (complete text of 1696).

Oeuvres. Ed. Julien Benda. Paris: Bibliothèque de la Pléiade, Gallimard, 1951. The most convenient modern edition of the complete works, with notes and variants.

Les Caractères. Ed. R. Garapon. Paris: Garnier, 1962. Complete text, notes, variants, glossary. The most convenient edition of the complete text; some controversial remarks on "burlesque" in the introduction.

Les Caractères. Ed. J. P. Kaminker. Paris: Larousse (Nouveaux Classiques Larousse), 1966, 2 vols. Excerpts for school use. Good notes, excellent glossary.

Les Caractères. Ed. Pierre Kuentz. Paris: Bordas (Selection Litteraire Bordas), 1969. Excerpts for school use. Excellent notes and commentary.

2. Translation

LA BRUYERE JEAN DE. *The Characters.* Trans. Jean Stewart. Baltimore: Penguin Books, 1970. The most readable translation. Good notes, very good introduction. Omits XIV, 48–51, and part of 52.

SECONDARY SOURCES

ADAM, ANTOINE. "La Bruyère" in *La fin de l'école classique 1680–1715*, Vol. V of *Histoire de la littérature française au xvii siècle* (Paris: Donat, 1956), 180–99. Primarily a seer and observer, La Bruyère's portrayal of manners extends to institutions and even to any society, but he is one of the religious moralists rather than a *philosophe*.

BARTHES, ROLAND. "La Bruyère," *Essais Critiques,* Paris: Seuil, 1964, pp. 221–37. Trans. Richard Howard, *Critical Essays,* Evanston: Northwestern University Press, 1972. *Caractère* as perception of concrete detail which expresses indirectly rather than didactically a conception of social reality.

BRODY, JULES. "Sur le style de La Bruyère," *Esprit Créateur* XI (Summer, 1971), 154–68. Style as expression of the *caractère's* superficiality and hollowness; physical expansion replaces and conceals the lack of reason and common sense.

DOUBROVSKY, SERGE. "Jean de La Bruyère," in *Explication de texte,* ed. Jean Sareil, Englewood Cliffs, N. J.: Prentice-Hall, 1970, I, 131–37. Physical detail, parallelism, symmetry, and variation in (VI, 83).

GOYET, MARIE-THERESE. "La composition d'ensemble du livre de La Bruyère," *Information littéraire* 7 (1955), 1–9. Arbitrary chapter titles as the least pretentious organization. Hierarchical presentation imitates society.

GUGGENHEIM, MICHEL. "L'homme sous le regard d'autrui ou le monde de La Bruyère," *PMLA* LXXXI (1966), 535–39. Man's social behavior is determined by others: seeing them and being seen by them.

HANKISS, JEAN. " 'Inspiration géométrique' dans les 'Caractères' de La Bruyère," *Neophilologus* 35 (1952), 65–75. Quantitative comparison, proportion, and antithesis as structures of the *moraliste* frame of reference.

HUDON, LOUIS. "La Bruyère et Montaigne," *Studi Francesi* 17 (1962), 208–24. Comparison of themes shows La Bruyère to be a mediocre and imitative moral philosopher.

JASINSKI, RENE. *Deux accès à La Bruyere.* Paris: Minard, 1971. Historical study of La Bruyère's adaptation of Theophrastus, the sources of XI–XIII, and the evolution of I–IV.

JEANSON, FRANCIS. "Le moraliste grandeur nature," *Les Temps modernes* No. 54 (avril, 1950), 1764–96. La Bruyère (pp. 1781–87) depicts and observes, but declines to analyze internal mechanisms and self-deceptions.

Selected Bibliography

KIRSCH, DORIS M. *"Style et vision du monde dans les Caractère de La Bruyère."* Diss. University of Rochester, 1971 (Ann Arbor: University Microfilms, No. 72–732). Detail, juxtaposition, and metaphors of the machine and the clock, show bourgeois materialism results in conditioning, despiritualization, and reification.

KOPPISCH, MICHAEL S. *"The Disappearance of Hypocrisy*: A Study of Changes in the Successive Editions of Les Caractères of Jean de La Bruyère." Diss. The Johns Hopkins University (Ann Arbor: University Microfilms, No. 70–26, 742). The work increasingly asserts a dependence of men on others for definition of what one is.

KRAILSHEIMER, A. J. "La Bruyère," *Studies in Self-Interest from Descartes to La Bruyère.* Oxford: Clarendon Press, 1962, pp. 196–208. La Bruyère opts for a bourgeois and mediocre solidarity, "controlled from above by a king ideally combining national, spiritual and personal authority" (p. 208).

LAUBRIET, PIERRE. "A propos des 'Caractères': ordre ou fantaisie?" *Revue d'histoire littéraire de la France* 67 (1967), 502–17. The fourth edition establishes the work's organization and harmony; man's natural state of corruption is the underlying idea.

MARMIER, JEAN. "Le Sens du mouvement chez La Bruyère," *Les Lettres romanes* XXI (1967), 223–37. Gesture, metaphors of movement, and antithesis show man shifting from one error to another.

MICHAUT, GUSTAVE. *La Bruyère.* Paris: Boivin, 1936. The first close and detailed study of La Bruyère as writer and social critic.

MILLY, JEAN ."La Bruyère: *Périandre* ou le parvenu," *Information littéraire* 18 (1966), 223–27. Composition, syntax, and choice of vocabulary in (VI, 21).

PAQUOT-PIERROT, LEON. *L'art du portrait chez La Bruyère.* Bruxelles: Collection Lebègue, 1941. Description, dramatization, and composition in the *caractère*.

PICARD, RAYMOND. "La Bruyère's *Caractères*," *Two Centuries of French Literature*. London: George Weidenfield and Nicolson, 1970, pp. 24–33. (Transl. of *Génie*

de la Littérature française, Paris: Hachette, 1970.)
Caractère as that which is characteristic. La Bruyère
as part of a tradition of essentialist psychology and
clssification.

RICHARD, PIERRE. *La Bruyère et ses "Caractères."* Paris:
Nizet, 1965. Biographical, historical, and critical study.

ROY, CLAUDE, ed. "Introduction aux *Caractères*" in *La Bruyère: Les Caractères.* Paris: Le Club Français du Livre,
1960, pp. 15–30. La Bruyère's social criticism is neither
original nor progressive; remarks on literary and social
posterity.

STEGMANN, ANDRE. *Les Caractères de La Bruyère,* Paris:
Larousse, 1972. Thorough and detailed, very good on
theme, language and technique. Appeared too late to
be considered in the present study.

TAVERA, FRANCOIS. *L'Idéal moral et l'idée religieuse dans les
Caractères de La Bruyère.* Paris: Mellottée, 1940. La
Bruyére's ideal is philosophical rather than religious:
the autonomous conscience and disinterested action.

VAN DELFT, LOUIS. *La Bruyère moraliste.* Genève: Droz,
1971. The evolution, composition, and world vision of
the *Characters.* As *moraliste,* compared to Castiglione
and Gracián.

VIROLLE, R. "La notion de 'vertu' dans les Caractères de La
Bruyère," *L'Ecole* 8 (1961), 327–30. *Virtue* is a lay
rather than religious term, akin to reason, dignity, and
the heart.

YARROW, P. J. "La Bruyère" in *The Seventeenth Century,*
Vol. II of P. E. Charvet, ed., *A Literary History of
France.* London: Ernest Benn Limited, 1967, 369–92.
Caractère as the study of man via portraits in action and
external details; review of themes and techniques.

Index

DATE DUE

GAYLORD			PRINTED IN U.S.A